Copyright by Gary North, 1992

Library of Congress Cataloging-in-Publication Data

North, Gary.

The Coase theorem : a study in economic epistemology / Gary North

p. cm.

Includes bibliographical references and index

ISBN 0-930464-61-3 (hardback : acid-free paper) $25.00

1. Economics – Moral and ethical aspects.
2. Pollution – Economic aspects.
3. Property.
4. Law – Economic aspects.
5. Coase, Ronald Harry   I. Title

HB72.N67 1992   91-40767
330.1–dc20   CIP

Institute for Christian Economics
P. O. Box 8000
Tyler, Texas 75711

This book is dedicated to

Brian Griffiths

academic economist, political advisor, and Christian moralist.

TABLE OF CONTENTS

Preface vii
Introduction 1

1. The Persistent Problem of Value 13
2. The Coase Theorem 23
3. Coase vs. Property Rights 36
4. Rothbard's Challenge to Coase 48
5. "Weighing Up the Gains and Losses" 63
6. The Crisis: Living With Dialectical Schizophrenia 87

Conclusion 97

Appendix 104
Bibliography 120
Index 123

In the development of any science, the first received paradigm is usually felt to account quite successfully for most of the observations and experiments easily accessible to that science's practitioners. Further development, therefore, ordinarily calls for the construction of elaborate equipment, the development of an esoteric vocabulary and skills, and a refinement of concepts that increasingly lessens their resemblance to their usual common-sense prototypes. That professionalization leads, on the one hand, to an immense restriction of the scientist's vision and to a considerable resistance to paradigm change. The science has become increasingly rigid. On the other hand, within those areas to which the paradigm directs the attention of the group, normal science leads to a detail of information and to a precision of the observation-theory match that could be achieved in no other way.

Thomas Kuhn*

---

*Thomas Kuhn, *The Structure of Scientific Revolutions* (Chicago: University of Chicago Press, 1962), p. 64.

PREFACE

> *Today in the sciences, books are usually either texts or retrospective reflections upon one aspect or another of the scientific life. The scientist who writes one is more likely to find his professional reputation impaired rather than enhanced.*
>
> Thomas Kuhn[1]

Science is a sacred cow, as Anthony Standen observed in 1950,[2] and modern economists are faithful academic hindus. They have done their best to hitch economics' wagon to the star of physical science. They have adopted physical science's use of mathematics, even when this methodological tool is totally inapplicable to the topic under discussion, which is most of the time in the study of individual human action. They have also imitated physical science's system of professional advancement by means of publishing scholarly articles in academic journals, meaning the top dozen or so professional journals.[3]

---

1. Thomas Kuhn, *The Structure of Scientific Revolutions* (Chicago: University of Chicago Press, 1962), p. 20.

2. Anthony Standen, *Science Is a Sacred Cow* (New York: Dutton, 1950).

3. John J. Siegfried, "The Publishing of Economic Papers and Its Impact on Graduate Faculty Ratings, 1960-1969," *Journal of Economic Literature*, X (1972), pp. 31-49. A. W. Coats writes: "In the process of acquiring his professional qualifications, every fledgling economist is initiated into the prevailing occupational folklore, part of which consists of opinions about the aims, characteristics, and comparative prestige ratings of the various periodical publications in the field. . . . [These opinions']

This is a book. It is not a scholarly article. Therefore, if Kuhn's comment is correct (and I believe it is), then the reader ought to conclude: (1) North is not trying to advance his professional career with this book; (2) North has no professional career to advance with this book; (3) North is a crap-shooter with his career; (4) economics is not a science; or (5) more than one of the above. Because so few economists have ever heard of me, any economist who stumbles across this book and then bothers to read it will probably prefer the first two choices. I can hardly disagree. But point four has a certain plausibility, at least in the opinion of non-economists. Still, formal discussion in the economics profession is conducted as if economics were a science, so we are driven back to points one through three.

In a very real sense, points one, two, and four are the case. This book presents a sustained argument against the claim of economists that economics is a hard science in the same sense that physics is a hard science. Economics is a difficult social science, but it is not a hard science. Why do I say this? For this reason: because of a crucial inconsistency in the epistemology of economics, virtually all of what passes today as economics cannot legitimately be regarded as scientific, given the presuppositions of economists. The better economists have recognized the existence of this epistemological Achilles heel for over half a century, but they have preferred to remain silent about it.

Epistemology

I am hard-pressed to think of any word better suited to reducing book sales among American academic economists than *epistemology*. (The more scientific sounding word, *methodology*, is only marginally more saleable.) American economists do not

---

importance should not be underestimated, for they constitute an essential part of the shared 'tacit knowledge' which is indispensable to the smooth functioning of the scientific communications network." A. W. Coats, "The Role of Scholarly Journals in the History of Economics: An Essay," *ibid.*, IX (1971), p. 39.

spend much time pondering epistemology's challenge: "What can I know and how can I know it?" At a symposium held at the annual meeting of the American Economic Association in 1951, Fritz Machlup identified the reality of the economics profession in the United States: "Usually only a small minority of American economists have professed interest in methodology. The large majority used to disclaim any interest in such issues."[4] In this regard, things have not changed much since 1951. Kuhn identifies two types of scientists: the "normal" practitioner and the revolutionary innovator. The typical normal practitioner of the economics profession has never even considered the issues that I discuss in this book.

Several years ago, a safely tenured economist at a large American state university assigned his graduate students an essay that I wrote in 1976. It dealt with the epistemological crisis of modern economics.[5] He reported to me that they resented having to read the essay. They did not want to be bothered by questions regarding the fundamental presuppositions of their life's work. They just wanted to get on with it.

This self-imposed blindness to questions of epistemology is, in the language of the profession, a product of rational self-interest. It is unwise to spend time pondering solutions to a problem that cannot be solved, given one's presuppositions, especially since any public discussion of this problem could reduce the demand for one's professional services. If I am correct about the epistemological weakness of all modern economic theory, and if economics is correct about the rational self-interest of acting individuals, then we should expect to

---

4. Fritz Machlup, "Introductory Remarks," *American Economic Review, Papers and Proceedings*, XLII (May 1952), p. 34. Note: the annual *Papers and Proceedings* issue of the *American Economic Review* is regarded by the profession as less relevant than publication in the other four issues of the *A.E.R.*: Siegfried, *op. cit.*, p. 34.

5. Gary North, "Economics: From Reason to Intuition," in North (ed.), *Foundations of Christian Scholarship: Essays in the Van Til Perspective* (Vallecito, California: Ross House, 1976).

encounter great resistance among professional economists concerning the question of epistemology.

What is the nature of the epistemological problem? From the marginalist (subjectivist) revolution of the 1870's until today, economists have faced a major dilemma: there is no known link that can be shown scientifically to connect the supposedly autonomous and totally subjective value scale of the individual decision-maker to the hypothetical, yet procedurally mandatory, aggregate known as social welfare or social utility. To make such comparisons, there must be a common value scale among all economic actors. No common value scale has ever been identified. The utilitarians' assumption of each person's equal capacity for happiness is merely that: an assumption.

Robbins vs. Harrod

This dilemma came into the open, briefly, in 1938, in a pair of essays by Lionel Robbins and Roy Harrod.[6] Robbins had cogently argued in his classic study, *An Essay on the Nature and Significance of Economic Science* (2nd ed., 1935), that it is scientifically impossible to make interpersonal comparisons of subjective utility. In other words, individual utility scales cannot be added up to produce a social aggregate. Social utility is therefore a scientific mirage. Harrod saw the inescapable implication of this position: it makes scientifically impossible any concept of applied economics. There is no way to discuss scientifically the social good or social welfare results of any policy, whether it was produced by a profit-seeking firm or by the State.

Harrod was logically correct regarding the implication of Robbins' thesis, as Robbins admitted a few months later, but Harrod's rejection of Robbins' epistemological position was not based on refuting either Robbins' premise – methodological

---

6. R. F. Harrod, "Scope and Method of Economics," *Economic Journal*, XLVIII (1938), especially pp. 396-97; Lionel Robbins, "Interpersonal Comparisons of Utility: A Comment," *ibid.*, especially pp. 635-41.

individualism – or his logic. It was based on his rejection of the inescapable implication of Robbins' postulate: the removal of all scientific content from policy-making. Harrod insisted that Robbins' conclusion was professionally unacceptable, not illogical.

Harrod was reviving the old dilemma raised by Jeremy Bentham: the aggregating of pleasure and pain in a world of hypothetically autonomous men. Bentham rejected any "anarchical" assumption that there are "as many standards of right and wrong as there are men," but on what basis was Bentham's rejection valid? As Halévy asked so many years ago: "But why is it necessary that a science of social man, based on a quantitative comparison of pleasures and pains, should be possible?" He pointed to the underlying flaw in Bentham's position: "But why does not the principle of utility enter, in the last analysis, into the class of 'anarchical' principles? Wherein does the notion of happiness, or of pleasure, necessarily imply, to use Bentham's expression, 'dimensions'? Can present pleasure be compared with past pleasure, which, by definition, no longer exists, or with future pleasure, which, by definition, does not yet exist? Can the pleasure experienced by one individual be compared with the pleasure of another individual?"[7] He cited Bentham's unpublished fragment, "Dimensions of Happiness":

> 'Tis in vain to talk of adding quantities which after the addition will continue distinct as they were before, one man's happiness will never be another man's happiness: a gain to one man is no gain to another: you might as well pretend to add twenty apples to twenty pears, which after you had done that could not be forty of any one thing but twenty of each just as there was before.[8]

---

7. Elie Halévy, *The Growth of Philosophical Radicalism*, translated by Mary Morris (1928) (Boston: Beacon, [1901-4] 1966), p. 495.

8. Bentham, "Dimension of Happiness," University College manuscripts; cited by Halévy, *idem*.

Bentham did not end his discussion at this point. If he had ended here, the *felicific calculus*, his theoretically essential intellectual construct, would have been stripped of all of its real-world content. Bentham needed this admittedly fictional aggregation: "This addibility of the happiness of different subjects, however, when considered rigorously, it may appear fictitious, is a postulatum without the allowance of which all political reasoning is at a stand. . . ."[9] Bentham saw clearly that social science, meaning the science that undergirds policy recommendations, must assume the ability of the policy-maker to add up the utilities of different individuals, even though the science of autonomous man says that this is an impossible task.

In the very next issue of the *Economic Journal*, Robbins backtracked. "But I confess that at first I found the implication very hard to swallow. For it meant, as Mr. Harrod rightly insisted, that economics as a science could say nothing by way of prescription."[10] This is exactly what it meant, and Robbins, too, was aghast. But not for long. "Further thought, however, convinced me that this was irrational." Why irrational? Because economists have always known that their prescriptions "were conditional upon the acceptance of norms lying outside economics. . . . Why should one be frightened, I asked, of taking a stand on judgements which are not scientific, if they relate to matters outside the world of science?"[11] Robbins returned epistemologically to Bentham's fiction of the common scale of utility, just as Harrod had.[12]

Robbins asked rhetorically why any economist should be frightened about such an appeal to standards lying outside of economic science. There is a very good reason why an academic

---

9. *Idem.*
10. Robbins, p. 637.
11. *Ibid.*, p. 638.
12. In 1961, Robbins cited Halévy's citations from Bentham: *The Theory of Economic Policy in English Classical Political Economy* (London: Macmillan, 1961), p. 180.

economist should be frightened: by appealing to ethical norms outside of the science of economics, he negates every trace of the scientific content of his policy recommendations and prescriptions. He thereby reduces economic policy-making to the level of – gasp! – political science, or even worse, sociology.

The exchange between Robbins and Harrod took place over half a century ago, yet the profession has politely buried all traces of it in its collective (!) memory. A few quirky people on the fringe of the profession resurrect this issue from time to time,[13] but the profession takes no notice. Nevertheless, just like Dracula, it cannot be permanently buried. It will continue to reappear, though perhaps only in the shadows, for as long as methodological individualism remains the official philosophical foundation of economic science. Given the rapid demise of the appeal of socialism since 1989, this foundation seems secure.

The Coase Theorem

The problem of making interpersonal comparisons of subjective utility lurks in the shadows of the classic essay by Ronald H. Coase, "The Problem of Social Cost."[14] The problem of the impossibility of making scientific comparisons of interpersonal subjective utility *is* the problem of social cost. Until it is dealt with forthrightly by Coase and his disciples, *the problem of social cost will remain the bedrock problem of modern economic science.* With the widespread acknowledgment after 1988 of the economic collapse of socialism in Eastern Europe and the USSR, and with the substitution of concern over pollution – the economic issue of "externalities" – as the justification for retaining political

---

13. Cf. Mark A. Lutz (economist) and Kenneth Lux (clinical psychologist), *The Challenge of Humanistic Economics* (Menlo Park, California: Benjamin/Cummings, 1979), ch. 5. The obscurity of both authors and their publisher is indicative of the problem: fringe critics. But their chapter is on target epistemologically and is a rhetorical delight to read.

14. R. H. Coase, "The Problem of Social Cost," *Journal of Law and Economics*, III (Oct. 1960), pp. 1-44.

control over the economy,[15] this problem is not likely to stay buried. I do my best in this monograph to keep it alive and healthy. I have thereby revealed my status as a fringe figure.

The Origin of This Monograph

The bulk of this monograph appeared as an appendix in my book, *Tools of Dominion: The Case Laws of Exodus* (1990).[16] In that form, it is available to few economists. Fewer still would be likely to discover the section in that book which deals with the Coase theorem on the economics of externalities (pollution, noise, and trespassing); the book is almost 1,300 pages long. This is why I decided to publish this modified version of my original analysis of the Coase theorem.

An added incentive to publish this monograph came as a result of Coase's winning of the Nobel Prize in economics in the fall of 1991. In a *Wall Street Journal* essay (Oct. 17, 1991), Kenneth Lehn summarized the Coase theorem and its impact on the economics profession. He wrote: "The 'problem' of externalities is not that one party causes harm to the other. Instead, the problem is one of conflict over how to use a scarce resource. In the case of air pollution, producers wish to use the air to emit pollutants while the neighboring residents wish to breathe fresh air. Using his legendary method of combing

---

15. Robert Heilbroner admitted in 1990 that Ludwig von Mises' critique of socialism in 1920 had been correct: socialist economic planning is inherently irrational. Oskar Lange's critique of Mises on this point was incorrect. Heilbroner, "Reflections: After Communism," *New Yorker* (Sept. 10, 1990), p. 92. He also admitted that socialism as an economic ideal went down with Communism's ship (pp. 98-99). But then he added this note of hope for all former socialists: "There is, however, another way of looking at, or for, socialism. It is to conceive of it not in terms of the specific improvements we would like it to embody but as the society that must emerge if humanity is to cope with the one transcendent challenge that faces it within a thinkable timespan. This is the ecological burden that economic growth is placing on the environment" (p. 99).

16. Gary North, *Tools of Dominion: The Case Laws of Exodus* (Tyler, Texas: Institute for Christian Economics, 1990), Appendix D: "The Epistemological Problem of Social Cost."

through court decisions, Prof. Coase went on to show that the 'problem' of externalities would be resolved, without government regulation, in ways that maximize social value if transaction costs are low, and the outcome does not depend on which party receives the initial property right." This is a misleading final sentence. There should have been a semicolon after the word *low*. It is the heart of the Coase theorem that the economic outcome does not depend on which party receives the initial property right. Mr. Lehn went on:

> "The Problem of Social Cost" spawned a large body of literature that debated the equilibrium tendencies of the imaginary world of zero transaction costs, a development that Prof. Coase found unfortunate. For the major insight of this paper was not to suggest that we live in this imaginary world, but rather to show conditions under which legal decisions concerning property rights do affect resource allocation.

I disagree. The article's major conclusion was that the initial distribution of property rights is economically irrelevant in establishing the social (aggregate) economic costs of settling disputes over externalities. If this thesis regarding costs of settling disputes over externalities is true, then R. H. Coase's theorem constitutes one of the most subtle yet profound attacks ever written on the concept of private property rights.

It is my perception of the subdiscipline of law and economics that it is dominated by scholars who have either accepted the truth of Coase's theorem or who have at least accepted its terms of discourse. To the extent that the field's developers have accepted the Coase theorem, this relatively recent academic subdiscipline is grounded on a concept of law which is at odds with the moral and legal foundations of liberty.

As I hope to show in this monograph, the Coase theorem is thoroughly consistent with the free market economic methodology associated with the Chicago School of economics. The Coase theorem on social cost is in this sense an example of the epistemological crisis of modern economics: grounded in the hypothetically value-neutral epistemology of modern economics, its conclusions are neither morally neutral nor consistent with the ideal of private property.

What I argue in this monograph is that the economics profession is suffering (though not financially) from a delusion. It is a widely shared delusion, and so is not discussed much or considered relevant in academic circles. This is to be expected: the inconsistencies that lie at the very heart of a widely shared delusion are seldom discussed, let alone taken seriously, by those who believe in the delusion. The economics profession's particular delusion – a commonly held one in contemporary scientific guilds – is the myth of neutrality. It undergirds the supposedly value-free methodology of economic science. It has manifested itself as a delusion in discussions, largely ignored, of the epistemological problem of making *scientifically valid* interpersonal comparisons of subjective utility. R. H. Coase's essay on social cost neglects even to mention this problem, yet the problem lies at the heart of that subdiscipline of economics known as welfare economics, in terms of which Coase's essay took shape.

That such a crucial aspect of welfare economics could be neglected in an essay that won the Nobel Prize for its author is evidence of the self-imposed blindness of the profession. That the field of law and economics, a recent subdiscipline of economics, grew to maturity in the soil – the cynic might say *nightsoil* – of Coase's theorem is even more astonishing.

With the publication of Coase's essay on social cost, the myth of moral neutrality in economics has ceased to be convenient. It has become a high-cost, low-return liability. Of course, I am speaking here of social costs and social convenience. For Coase, both the essay and the myth that undergirds it have proven to be a bonanza, both professionally and financially. Professor Coase won a million dollars for two essays: "The Nature of the

Firm" (1937) and "The Problem of Social Cost" (1960).[17] These articles gained him tenure in one of the most prestigious and well-remunerated economics departments on earth. He wrote other articles, of course: "Bacon Production and the Pig Cycle in Great Britain" (1935), "The Pig Cycle: A Rejoinder" (1935), "The Pig Cycle in Great Britain: An Explanation" (1937), and, of course, "Rowland Hill and the Penny Post" (1939). But he is not renowned for these, nor for his one book, published in 1950, in a career that exceeds half a century. Coase's career provides evidence (admittedly anecdotal) that Kuhn's statement, cited at the beginning of this Preface, is correct: the pathway to professional success within any academic scientific guild today is the journal article, not the book.

Warning

Let the reader beware: I am a Bible-believing Christian. I have self-consciously used biblical presuppositions regarding ethics and responsibility, both personal and corporate, in order to form my negative judgment regarding the "net social cost" of Coase's theorem. I have also invoked the epistemological insights of the Austrian School economist Murray Rothbard in dissecting the epistemological problem of collective judgments and collective value. This no doubt will place the academic mark of Cain on my forehead. To invoke the Bible positively and Rothbard negatively in order to make judgments regarding the validity of economic science is, in the eyes of a modern economist, the only known practice more reprehensible professionally than invoking sociology.

---

17. Only these two essays were cited by the Royal Swedish Academy. Peter Pasell, "Economics Nobel to a Basic Thinker," *New York Times* (Oct. 16, 1991).

If a man shall cause a field or vineyard to be eaten, and shall put in his beast, and shall feed in another man's field; of the best of his own field, and of the best of his own vineyard, shall he make restitution. If fire break out, and catch in thorns, so that the stacks of corn, or the standing corn, or the field, be consumed therewith; he that kindled the fire shall surely make restitution.

Exodus 22:5-6

The traditional approach has tended to obscure the nature of the choice that has to be made. The question is commonly thought of as one in which A inflicts harm on B and what has to be decided is: how should we restrain A? But this is wrong. We are dealing with a problem of a reciprocal nature. To avoid the harm to B would inflict harm on A. The real question that has to be decided is: should A be allowed to harm B or should B be allowed to harm A? The problem is to avoid the more serious harm.

R. H. Coase*

---

*R. H. Coase, "The Problem of Social Cost." *Journal of Law and Economics*, III (Oct. 1960), p. 2.

INTRODUCTION

Costs and benefits cannot be compared across individuals, even when monetary sums are involved, because of the impossibility of interpersonal utility comparison. This insight is a straightforward application of the defining principle of the Austrian school: radical subjectivism.[1]

Since all costs and benefits are subjective, no government can accurately identify, much less establish, the optimum quantity of anything. But even the tort [private law suit over wrongs – G.N.] approach runs up against the immeasurability of costs and benefits: how are damages to be determined?[2]

Another problem is the lack of a method for calculating the effect of a decision or policy on the total happiness of the relevant population. Even within just the human population, there is no reliable technique for measuring a change in the level of satisfaction of one individual relative to a change in the level of satisfaction of another.[3]

Economists are a cynical bunch. What is a cynic? I do not mean the Greek definition. A modern economist would regard

---

1. John B. Egger, "Comment: Efficiency Is Not a Substitute for Ethics," in Mario Rizzo (ed.), *Time, Uncertainty, and Disequilibrium* (Lexington, Massachusetts: Lexington Books, 1979), p. 121. Italics not in original.
2. Charles W. Baird, "The Philosophy and Ideology of Pollution Regulation," *Cato Journal*, II (Spring 1982), p. 303. Italics not in original.
3. Richard A. Posner, *The Economics of Justice* (Cambridge, Massachusetts: Harvard University Press, 1983), p. 54. Italics not in original.

the cynic Diogenes' search for an honest man – a man whose support could not be purchased – as a wasteful expenditure of scarce economic resources. Economists know before they begin – begin anything – that "every person has his price." There are therefore no truly honest men. I have in mind rather the definition of the cynic that was offered by Oscar Wilde in *Lady Windermere's Fan*: "A man who knows the price of everything and the value of nothing" – the economist as cynic.

The economist's dilemma – the dilemma of value vs. price – is in fact the central dilemma of the academic discipline known as economics. Economists search for an answer to one question above all other questions: "What is the verifiable relationship between value and price?" For over two centuries, generations of economists have attempted to discover the answer, and it eludes them today as much as it did in the days of Adam Smith. The difference is, today the lack of any internally consistent answer is covered by far more layers of dead ends that were and are described as successful solutions to the problem.

Value and Price

Let us begin the search. Assume that you are interrogating a modern economist. You ask: If all value is objective, then why do prices keep changing? What is it that makes them change? Answer: *Supply and demand change.* Why does supply change? *In response to changes in demand.* Why does demand change? *Because people change their minds.* Why? *Because prices change.* Why do prices change? *Changing conditions of supply and demand.*

Wait a minute. We are going in circles. We had better talk about demand apart from price. *Sorry, you are not allowed to talk about demand apart from price, or price apart from demand.* All right, let me ask this: If people's changing minds are the source of the changes in demand, then isn't the price of anything really based on subjective value? *Yes, that is correct.* Personal subjective value? *Yes, that is correct.* But how is personal subjective value translated into objective value? *It isn't; there is no objective value.*

Well, then, how is personal subjective value translated into objective prices? *Through competitive bidding.*

This leads to another series of questions. You ask: How can we be sure that the outcome of the objective individual bids reflects the true value to society? *By denying that there is any true value to society apart from the outcome of the objective individual bids.* But what if society disagrees? *There is no such thing as society; there are only individuals.* But what if individuals vote to change the outcome? *That is their legal privilege in a democracy.* Are you saying that democracy is a valid way to achieve social goals? *I am an economist; I can only tell you the outcome of events, given certain causes.* Should democracies vote to change the outcome of the bids? *I am an economist; there is no ultimate "should" for an economist.*

You press your case: What is the value of economics? *Sorry; economics does not objectively exist; only economists exist.* What is an economist? *An economist is someone who does economics.* I see. Well, then, what is the value of an economist? *That must be determined subjectively.* All right, what is the price of an economist? *All the market will bear.* Are we paying economists too much? *The free market will decide that.* Do we have a free market in economists today? *I'd prefer not to say; I might get fired. I work for a state university. It is not in my self-interest to answer your question.*

In my view, the answer is clear: yes, we are paying economists too much. Is my view correct? That *is* the question.

In this monograph, I intend to show that all of modern economics is a gigantic intellectual fraud, an illusion so successful that the vast majority of its practitioners are not aware of the fraud which they are perpetrating. I will show that the procedures that economists say they use are not the ones they actually use, that the presuppositions they say they have adopted are not actually the ones they have adopted, and that their ability to make economic judgments is in fact denied by their very methodology. All you have to do is read the entire monograph, paying attention to my arguments as you read.

Am I overstating my case? *You cannot know for sure until you read it.* Is it worth the risk – the time, energy, and mental effort – to find out? *Only you can say, and only after you read it.*

Only you! Therein lies the epistemological problem for modern economics.

To Read or Not to Read

What will it cost you to read this essay? You will never know for sure. It is analogous to a far more important question in life, "What will it cost me to marry this person?" Both questions really mean: "What will I have to give up forever?" While the "foreverness" of the marriage decision is more obvious to us – "till death do us part" is a graphic covenantal phrase – the "foreverness" of every decision is analogous, though not of the same order of magnitude.

When I choose *this* rather than *that*, I forever forfeit *that*, as well as all the little thats which might have been born later on. Perhaps I can change my mind later on, and buy *that*, but it will not be the same *that* which I choose not to buy today. It is a later *that*. Like a high school sweetheart whom you marry only after your first spouse dies, time has worked its changes on both of you. Everything a person might have accomplished with *that* during the period of "*this* rather than *that*" is gone forever.

A Fork in the Road

We know that in making any decision, we must forfeit many things that might have been but will never be – indeed, a whole lifetime of things that might have been – but we never know exactly what. Every decision, moment by moment, is to some extent the proverbial fork in the road. We do not know the next twenty moves and counter-moves in a chess game – moves that will become reality *in part* because of the next move – so it is safe to say that we cannot know what life has in store for us when we do one thing today rather than another.

If you read this essay, it is because you think it will be "worth your time." But what is your time worth? What is your time worth right now? It is worth whatever is the most valuable use to which you can put it. What is the cost of spending your time one way rather than another? The most valuable use foregone. So, what is your decision? "To read or not to read, that is the question!"

Decisions, decisions. Once our decision is made, we put the past irrevocably behind us. "The moving finger writes, and having written, moves on." We then face the consequences of our decision. But these consequences – these *costs* – are imposed on us after the decision, not before. They are costs, but they are not costs that affected the original action. *Expected* costs affected the original action, not the actual costs that we in fact subsequently experience. Is this unclear? Ask the person who married the "wrong" spouse to explain the difference between expected costs and resulting costs. Nobel-Prize winning economist James Buchanan distinguishes between two kinds of costs: choice-*influencing* costs and choice-*influenced* costs.[4]

Unmeasurable Costs

Choice-influencing costs are inherently unmeasurable by any scientific standard. The economist insists that, like beauty in the eyes of the beholder, these economic costs exist only in the mind of the decision-maker. They are subjectively perceived, and *only* subjectively perceived. And yet, and yet . . . there really are beautiful women and ugly women, and just about everyone can discern the difference, including the respective women (*especially* the women). But how is this possible? How can we deny the objective reality of beauty in the name of a "higher" subjective reality, when we know that in order for our

---

4. James Buchanan, *Cost and Choice: An Inquiry in Economic Theory* (Chicago: University of Chicago Press, 1969), pp. 44-45. Buchanan won the Nobel Prize in 1986.

subjective appraisals to have meaning, there had better be an objective reality undergirding them? After all, two and two make four. Or do they? Does the objective answer depend on the subjective evaluator? The modern mathematician is not really sure.[5]

The costs that influence our decisions are always subjective evaluations of future potential consequences. This is Buchanan's argument. Once we act, however, objective reality takes over, replacing our mental forecasts with cold, hard facts. (And yet, and yet . . . in order to be perceived by us, these cold, hard facts must first be warmed in the microwave ovens of our minds.) Thus, concludes Buchanan: "Costs that are influential for behavior do not exist; they are never realized; they cannot be measured after the fact."[6] The dream becomes reality, but the reality is always different from the dream, at least to this extent: the dream could not be measured; the reality can be. Supposedly.

Buchanan argues that the choice-influenced costs that are subsequently imposed on people as a result of some previous decision are in some sense objective and measurable – so many forfeited dollars of income, for example[7] – but these real-world costs did not affect the original decision in any way. Yet even this doffing of the economist's cap to objective cost theory may be overly respectful, given the presuppositions of modern subjectivist economics. What do the numbers mean? The *meaning* of these objective, choice-influenced costs – e.g., accounting costs – must be *subjectively evaluated* by the person who bears them. A number in a ledger is supposed to convey accurate and

---

5. Vern Poythress, "A Biblical View of Mathematics," in Gary North (ed.), *Foundations of Christian Scholarship: Essays in the Van Til Perspective* (Vallecito, California: Ross House, 1976), pp. 159-88.

6. Buchanan, *Cost and Choice*, p. vii.

7. Even here, who can be sure just how many dollars were actually forfeited as a result of the decision? Would the person's *perceived* alternative use of his money have been as wise (high return) as the best opportunity the market *objectively* offered at the time?

economically relevant information in order for it to be effective as a summary of past events. The individual who pays an accountant thinks he is getting something for his money. What is he getting? A bunch of numbers on a page? Or information? The individual must interpret the significance of this choice-inflencing information. There is no escape from subjectivism.

The Roads Untravelled

Consider your own situation. You are still reading this essay. You still have faith in a positive future return on your present investment of time. Let us consider a hypothetical possibility. With the time you spend reading this essay (assuming you stick with it to the bitter end), you might be able to think of an investment strategy that would make you rich, but because of something you will read here, you will never think of it or have the courage to risk it. On the other hand, you may also avoid an investment that really would bankrupt you. Unlike the man in the story of the lady and the tiger, you have the option of ignoring both doors; instead, you choose to read this essay. But you could have opened a door. Which would it have been, the lady or the tiger? You cannot know for sure. You will never know. You can only guess. So, what is the true cost of reading this essay? Life with the lady or a brief but colorful encounter with the tiger?

If we take seriously the modern economist's discussion of costs and choices, we may find our world disturbing. We never really know what our actions are costing us, assuming that it is true that there is no way to relate our subjective evaluations before we act with objective costs after we act. This disturbing lack of certainty can be relieved by an act of faith: "And we know that all things work together for good to them that love God, to them who are the called according to his purpose" (Romans 8:28). But this providential word of encouragement is hardly helpful to the modern humanistic economist.

We can of course sit around moaning and groaning about a past cost: the abandoned dream that might have come true. We can worry retroactively about what our decision has cost us. But the cost that really counted – "counted" is in fact misleading, since there was nothing objective to count – at the moment of our decision was imposed at that moment. What is past is past. Paul wrote: ". . . forgetting those things which are behind, and reaching forth unto those things which are before" (Philippians 3:13). This is what the economist says of all decisions. Decision-makers are necessarily forward-looking. The past is completely gone forever. We must do the best we can with whatever we have today. This is the doctrine of *sunk costs*.[8]

This is not to say that we do not bear the objective costs that are imposed by a previous decision. We do. Even if we do not perceive these costs, we bear them. A madman may not understand that he is not Napoleon, but he bears the social costs of his delusion when he is placed in an insane asylum. This is why there can be no escape from objective costs, any more than from subjective costs. But whether we accurately foresaw these costs or not, they are the *result* of that action, not its cause. These costs are borne by us objectively in history, yet they are always subjectively borne. One person may bear his burden in good cheer; another is utterly oppressed by what objectively (i.e., to an outside evaluator) appears to be the same magnitude of burden. Who is to say whose evaluation is correct? The Christian answers: only the omniscient God can do this, and His evaluation is not objectively measurable by the economist. Remove His evaluation from the discussion of imputed value, and the world explodes in a kaleidoscope of subjective evaluations.[9] This is the epistemological dilemma of modern man.

---

8. Gary North, *An Introduction to Christian Economics* (Nutley, New Jersey: Craig Press, 1973), ch. 26: "Urban Renewal and the Doctrine of Sunk Costs."

9. On kaleidic imputations, see the works of G. L. S. Shackle and Ludwig M. Lachmann.

Some Odd Conclusions

An exclusively subjectivist view of cost and choice can lead to some very odd conclusions. (So, for that matter, can any other exclusive line of human reasoning.) G. F. Thirlby follows the logic of an individual's one-time decision. He concludes: "Cost is ephemeral. The cost involved in a particular decision loses its significance with the making of a decision because the decision displaces the alternative course of action."[10] He says emphatically that "the cost figure will never become objective, i.e. it will never be possible to check whether the forecast of the alternative revenue was correct, because the alternative undertaking will never come into existence to produce the *actual* alternative revenue."[11] This is Buchanan's conclusion, too. But if no cost ever becomes objective, what is the purpose of accounting?

Should You Fire Your Accountant?

What does all this mean for the accounting profession? What does it do to the very concept of personal or corporate budgeting? He does not say, but he does not stop, either. Following the persuasive logic of subjectivism, Thirlby concludes that "The cost is not the things – e.g., *money – which will flow along certain channels* as a result of the decision; it is a loss, prospective or otherwise, to the person making the decision, of the opportunity of using those things in the alternative course of action. A fortiori, this cost *cannot be discovered by another person who eventually watches and records the flow of those things along those channels.*"[12] Then of what objective use are accountants? Why was

---

10. G. F. Thirlby, "The Subjective Theory of Value and Accounting Cost," *Economica*, XII (Feb. 1946); reprinted in James Buchanan and G. F. Thirlby (eds.), *L.S.E. Essays on Cost* (New York: New York University Press, 1981), p. 140. L.S.E. stands for London School of Economics.

11. Thirlby, "The Ruler," *South African Journal of Economics*, XIV (Dec. 1946), p. 264; *ibid.*, p. 182.

12. Thirlby, "Subjective Theory," *ibid.*, p. 139.

the advent of double-entry bookkeeping such a revolutionary event in the history of civilization?[13] He does not say.

Furthermore, what does such a view of budgeting do to the idea of the free market as a social institution for producing economic order – *objective* economic order? What does such a view do to the idea of the stock market, since money prices for shares are the means by which decision-makers evaluate the past performance of all other participants in the market? What does the price of a share of corporate stock have to do with expected future performance of that corporation's management? What is the link, if any, between present share prices and future economic performance? How do we get from subjective value to objective share prices and back again? How do we preserve our capital? For that matter, how do we measure our capital? How can we bridge the gap between the world of (1) exclusively subjective costs and (2) objective market prices? Buchanan insists: "*Only prices have objective, empirical content. . . .*"[14] Then precisely what empirical content does a price possess or reveal, and how do we discover it or make effective use of it – subjectively and objectively, personally and socially?

In short, what does an objective price have to do with individual subjective value? What is the *economic meaning* of a price – individually and socially, subjectively and objectively? (This is the number-one epistemological problem that has beset modern economics since the 1870's.)

The Realm of Possibility

Consider another example. Buchanan makes this statement: "Any profit opportunity that is within the realm of possibility but which is rejected becomes a cost of undertaking the pre-

---

13. Ludwig von Mises, *Human Action: A Treatise on Economics* (3rd ed.; Chicago: Regnery, 1966), p. 230. Published originally by Yale University Press in 1949.
14. Buchanan, *Cost and Choice*, p. 85.

ferred course of action."[15] But Buchanan neglects any consideration of the economics of a rejected opportunity that is not in fact – *objective* fact – within the realm of possibility. We normally call such an opportunity a *loss*. Wouldn't avoiding it be a *benefit* of undertaking the preferred course of action? If the decision-maker's first choice is to reject the objectively impossible (i.e., unprofitable) course of action for whatever reason, and also to reject the second, objectively possible, course of action for whatever reason, won't he remain in the profit column overall? I do not want to press this line of reasoning too hard because it bogs us down too deeply in the philosophical problem of available and unavailable information, but we need to recognize at least the nature of the epistemological problem: *If everything is completely subjective at the moment of decision, what does "the realm of possibility" have to do with anything?* Maybe the decision-maker believes that can achieve something great if he just had the courage of his convictions, when in fact the action will bankrupt him. Is his true cost the forfeited unattainable greatness or the forfeited inevitable bankruptcy? If all costs at the time of his decision are purely subjective, then his cost must be the forfeited greatness. This, clearly, is nutty – logical but nutty. So is any theory of cost and choice that is exclusively subjective.

The economist, no matter how hard he tries to tie human decisions exclusively to the action-taker's subjective evaluations, cannot escape the bedrock realm of possibility. This is his true measuring rod for discussing cost, the *ruler* without which all economic discussion becomes theoretically impossible. On the other hand, no matter how hard he tries to make objective that realm of possibility, through probability theory and other statistical techniques, he cannot escape the inherent subjectivity of the decision of the acting individual who is responsible for his actions. The economist needs – yes, *needs*[16] – a scientific theory

---

15. *Ibid.*, p. 28.
16. Few concepts are less acceptable to an economist that the concept of *need*. A

of cost that is both subjective and objective without being eternally dialectical. Such a theory does not exist in the world of humanistic economics. This is the heart of my critique of all previous discussions of the problem of social cost.

Conclusion

The epistemological problem of value has bothered economists from the early days of the discipline's development. Is value objective, subjective, or a combination? Is it imputed? If so, by whom? Who is the voice of authority who decides the question: "What is this worth?" How do we decide as individuals what anything is worth? How do we decide collectively? For we must decide collectively if we are to deal institutionally and legally with the problem of *externalities* (e.g., air pollution), which is closely related to the problem of social cost.

R. H. Coase believes that he has discovered the theoretical basis for discovering practical answers to these questions. The Nobel Committee seems to agree with him. To evaluate the net social value of Coase's theorem, we need first to examine in greater detail the details of the debate over economic value that has been going on in the economics profession from the beginning, but especially since 1938.

I use Coase's essay as a representative example of almost the entire economics profession. I argue in this monograph that Coase's unstated presupposition is mythological, namely, the ideal of moral neutrality in economic science. The ideal of neutrality has been dominant in the academic discipline of economics ever since the late seventeenth century.[17] It has served as a professionally convenient myth from the beginning. It will not be surrendered at zero price or zero cost.

---

need is something which is not negotiable, and for an economist, everything economic is defined as negotiable.

17. William Letwin, *The Origins of Scientific Economics* (Cambridge, Massachusetts: M.I.T. Press, 1963). Paperback edition by Doubleday, 1965.

1

THE PERSISTENT PROBLEM OF VALUE

In both political and scientific development the sense of malfunction that can lead to crisis is prerequisite to revolution.

Thomas Kuhn[1]

Economists, as self-consciously humanistic social scientists, claim to be defenders of a rational academic discipline. Most of them defend their methodology in terms of the assertion that it allows them to make accurate predictions of human actions under limited, specified conditions.[2] These predictions are supposed to enable people to make economic decisions that are more profitable than decisions made by flipping a coin, consulting a fortune teller, or throwing darts at a wall covered with slips of paper, with each slip containing a different suggested course of action.

To make their claim believable, economists have to make a myriad of assumptions about reason, the human mind, the powers of observation, the external world, and the interrela-

---

1. Thomas Kuhn, *The Structure of Scientific Revolutions* (Chicago: University of Chicago Press, 1962), p. 91.
2. Milton Friedman, *Essays in Positive Economics* (Chicago: University of Chicago Press, 1953), ch. 1: "The Methodology of Positive Economics."

tionships between the mind and matter. These assumptions are very seldom spelled out by economists.[3] Epistemology, the fundamental question of all philosophy – "What can man know, and how can he know it?" – is not a popular topic within the economics profession.

The Problem of Measurement

The advent of modern economics is generally dated from the early 1870's, when three scholars independently came to the same conclusion, namely, that economic value is *imputed*: the concept of *subjective* value.[4] Value, they concluded, is subjectively determined. It is not an objective quantity. The key unit of value is the value (subjective) of the marginal unit. The decision-maker asks himself: How much (objectively) of *this* must I give up in order to obtain *that*? By 1900, virtually all non-Marxist economists had broken with the older objective value theories of the classical economists, such as the labor theory of value or the cost-of-production theory of value. By grounding economics on the subjective valuations of individual decision-makers, economists today believe that they have escaped from the intellectual dilemmas that had arisen as a result of classical economics' objective value theory. (The most famous one was Adam Smith's "water-diamond paradox.")[5]

---

3. Gary North, "Economics: From Reason to Intuition," in North (ed.), *Foundations of Christian Scholarship* (Vallecito, California: Ross House, 1976).

4. The three scholars were William Stanley Jevons (England), Carl Menger (Austria), and Leon Walras (Switzerland). See R. S. Hovey, *The Rise of the Marginal Utility School, 1870-1889* (Lawrence: University of Kansas Press, 1960); Emil Kauder, *A History of Marginal Utility* (Princeton, New Jersey: Princeton University Press, 1965).

5. "The things which have the greatest value in use have frequently little or no value in exchange. . . . Nothing is more useful than water: . . . A diamond, on the contrary, has scarce any value in use; . . ." Adam Smith, *Wealth of Nations* (1776), end of Chapter IV. The paradox: Why is it that something as valuable to human life as water is worth so little in comparison to diamonds, which are not really crucial to mankind? The marginalist-subjectivist's solution: "We never choose between water in general and diamonds in general. We choose between a specific amount of water and a specific amount of diamonds at a specific point in time. In the middle of a desert,

They are self-deluded. They have not escaped such problems. They have merely created new intellectual problems for themselves – problems that are inescapable, given their commitment to the ancient ideal of humanism: "man as the measure of all things" (Protagoras).[6] (The careful economist would add this cautious corollary: "assuming for the sake of argument that there can be such a thing as a measure in economics.")

If man is the measure of all things, and man himself is a subjective, changing, and ultimately "free spirit," then "man" cannot serve as a measure of anything. Measures must be fixed, but there are no remaining fixed measures in modern thought – not even the speed of light (at least in quantum physics).[7] They are no longer fixed in biology: Darwinism's world of process has triumphed over fixed measures.[8] Measures are no longer fixed in morals.[9] They are no longer fixed in epistemology.[10] They do not exist in economics.[11] There are no mea-

---

someone might buy a canteen of water with a bag of diamonds. Under most circumstances, he wouldn't. Water is abundant compared to diamonds most of the time. Thus, the decision-maker's subjective evaluation at a particular moment of time is crucial, not the hypothetical (and non-existent) objective value of water in general vs. the objective value of diamonds in general."

6. Assertion 5 of Humanist Manifesto I (1933) states: "Humanism asserts that the nature of the universe depicted by modern science makes unacceptable any supernatural or cosmic guarantees of human values." *Humanist Manifestos I and II* (Buffalo, New York: Prometheus Press, 1973), p. 8.

7. I refer here to the startling theory of subatomic physics, verified by numerous experiments, known as Bell's Theorem, which states that at the subatomic level, all events must be simultaneously related to each other across the entire universe. See Nick Herbert, *Quantum Reality: Beyond the New Physics* (Garden City, New York: Anchor Press/Doubleday, 1985), p. 214.

8. Assertion 2 of Humanist Manifesto I states: "Humanism believes that man is a part of nature and that he has emerged as the result of a continuous process." *Humanist Manifestos I and II*, p. 8.

9. Forty years later, Humanist Manifesto II stated: "Ethics is *autonomous* and *situational*, needing no theological or ideological sanction. Ethics stems from human need and interest." *Ibid.*, p. 17.

10. Delwin Brown, Ralph E. James, and Gene Reeves (eds.), *Process Philosophy and Christian Thought* (Indianapolis: Bobbs-Merrill, 1971).

11. Ludwig von Mises writes: "The truth is that there are only variables and no

sures at all. There may be discrete, permanent numbers – even this is highly speculative[12] – but there are no measures. Everything is on a continuum, nothing is discrete.[13] This absence of measures leads, step by step, to radical subjectivism and radical relativism. Heraclitus' river of historical flux is clearly eroding Parmenides' fixed logical shore line. Chaos looms.[14]

Having said this, the economist nevertheless resists making the obvious conclusion regarding the relativity of all measurement: *the denial of the possibility of relevant scientific precision.* In vain, the economist protests: "There are economists who have propounded the relativity of measure. Apparently, they failed to see that this view saps the entire foundation upon which the economic science rests."[15] He, too, is inescapably one of these epistemologically short-sighted economists.

Consider the question of environmental pollution. The consistent economist must conclude something like the following: "One man's polluted stream is another man's profit for the fiscal year, and there is no conceivable scientific way to say which is better for society in general, for there is no scientific way of identifying such an entity as society in general." This is the logic of subjective value theory. To admit this, however, would be to commit methodological suicide in public. Modern economics has in fact committed suicide, but it has done so in private. Economists do not leap from tall buildings during the lunch hour. They much prefer to do away with themselves in

---

constants. It is pointless to talk of variables where there are no invariables." Mises, *Theory and History: An Interpretation of Social and Economic Evolution* (New Haven, Connecticut: Yale University Press, 1957), p. 13. This was reprinted by the Mises Institute in 1985.

12. Vern Poythress, "A Biblical View of Mathematics," in North (ed.), *Foundations of Christian Scholarship*, ch. 9.

13. Nicholas Georgescu-Roegen, *The Entropy Law and the Economic Process* (Cambridge, Massachusetts: Harvard University Press, 1971), ch. 3.

14. James Gleick, *Chaos: Making a New Science* (New York: Viking, 1987).

15. Georgescu-Roegen, *Entropy Law*, p. 111.

private – through an overdose of qualifications. As they depart from this life, each proclaims a unique theory of value.

The Great Debate

In *The Dominion Covenant: Genesis*, I discussed at considerable length the problem of objective and subjective value. I analyzed the important critique of Cambridge Professor A. C. Pigou by London School of Economics Professor Lionel Robbins, and then the subsequent debate in 1938 between Robbins and Roy Harrod.[16] To review very briefly, Pigou, in his pioneering study of welfare economics, had argued that since each additional monetary unit's worth of income is worth less to a man than the previous unit, the value of one additional unit of income to a millionaire will necessarily be less than its value to a poverty-stricken man. Thus, Pigou concluded, the State can increase the aggregate social welfare of the community by taking a portion of the rich man's income in the high income brackets and transferring this money to the poor man. This tax will not hurt the rich man very much (he puts so little value on the last bit of money he receives), while the marginal income will greatly benefit the poor man (who has so little income to begin with). For several decades, this argument was considered a valid scientific defense of the graduated income tax.

Robbins replied in 1932 that the argument is invalid as a scientific statement. Since all value is subjective, we cannot, as scientists, make interpersonal comparisons of subjective utility. There is no objective column of figures to add up when we are talking about subjective value. (Conclusion: the technique of accounting can have no logical connection with either the so-called science of economics or the vocation of business. This is the epistemological issue that I raised in the Introduction.)[17]

---

16. Gary North, *The Dominion Covenant: Genesis* (2nd ed.; Tyler, Texas: Institute for Christian Economics, 1987), ch. 4.

17. See Appendix, below, "There's No (Autonomous) Accounting for Taste."

Therefore, economists cannot legitimately say anything about any increase or decrease of "social value" which is produced by taking a percentage of the rich man's income in the higher brackets and giving this money to the poor man.[18]

No defender of subjectivist (marginalist) economics has been able to refute Robbins' argument, yet hardly any economist – I would say no economist – has been able to develop a comprehensive economic theory in terms of his argument, including Robbins.[19] Robbins destroyed the epistemological foundation of applied economics.

Roy Harrod[20] complained in his rejoinder in 1938 that if Robbins were really serious about this argument, then he would have to abandon the idea that it is possible for the economist, as a scientist, to make *any* recommendations concerning proper

---

18. Lionel Robbins, *An Essay on the Nature and Significance of Economic Science* (2nd ed.; New York: St. Martins, [1935]).

19. Writes Richard Posner: "The 'interpersonal comparison of utilities' is anathema to the modern economist, and rightly so, because there is no metric for making such a comparison." Had he let it go at that, he would have been honest. But he knows what this would mean: the impossibility of formulating any social policy based on truly scientific economics, so he illegitimately adds the following unproven and unprovable statement: "But the interpersonal comparison of values, in the economic sense, is feasible, although difficult, even when the values are not being compared in an explicit market." Richard A. Posner, *The Economics of Justice* (Cambridge, Massachusetts: Harvard University Press, 1983), p. 79. Apparently, all the economist needs to do is change the word "utility" to "values," and he goes from the impossible to the merely difficult. Let me tell you something about humanistic economists: *they cheat.* Maybe not self-consciously, but the resulting confusion is the same. At the very least, the economics profession is self-deceived.

20. Harrod later became Sir Roy Harrod. He was John Maynard Keynes' handpicked successor as editor of *The Economic Journal.* Together, they controlled access to England's most prestigious academic economics journal for half a century. Like Keynes, he never received an academic degree in economics. He did study economics with Keynes for one year, 1922-23. Neither of them ever earned a degree above the bachelor's degree: Keynes' was in mathematics and Harrod's was in the humanities. See Don Patinkin, *Anticipations of the General Theory? And Other Essays on Keynes* (Chicago: University of Chicago Press, 1982), pp. xv, xvi. John Neville Keynes, Maynard's father, and Pigou personally paid for young Maynard's salary when they hired him to teach economics at King's College, Cambridge in 1908. Keynes, Sr. was chairman of the department for many years.

economic policy, since any policy always hurts some participants and benefits others. If it is impossible to make interpersonal comparisons of subjective utility, then economists must remain forever silent about the aggregate (social) economic benefits and costs of any decision by an individual or by the State.[21]

Robbins was correct in his criticism of Pigou, given the presuppositions of modern, subjectivist economics. Harrod was equally correct in his criticism of Robbins, namely, that *his conclusion, if accepted, would destroy all applied economic science.* Robbins subsequently backed away from this conclusion concerning the inability of economists to say anything about social welfare or the benefits of social policies in general.[22] But he never explained how he could logically back away from this conclusion, and he had over four additional decades to provide the explanation. Even more inconsistently, he also never backed away from his critique of Pigou's argument in favor of graduated ("progressive") income taxation.

The implications of Robbins' position are radical, and economists have long been unwilling to face them, including Robbins. Buchanan once wrote that "it is precisely the problems posed in modern welfare economics that force the economist to come to grips with the basic issues of political and legal philosophy."[23] These issues also force the more astute economist to come to grips with the fundamental issue of all philosophy: *epistemology*. But the ranks of the economics profession are filled with men and women who have no training in epistemology and care nothing about it.[24] They never answer by means of modern subjectivism the fundamental philosophical question: "What can

---

21. R. F. Harrod, "Scope and Method of Economics," *Economic Journal*, XLVIII (1938), p. 397.

22. Lionel Robbins, "Interpersonal Comparisons of Utility: A Comment," *ibid.*, pp. 635-37.

23. James Buchanan, "Good Economics – Bad Law," *Virginia Law Review*, LX (1974), p. 488.

24. An exception is the Austrian School.

men know, and how can they know it?" They operate in terms of an implicit though hidden dialecticism between objective and subjective value theory.

Social Cost

Pigou also raised another issue concerning welfare economics. It is a variant of the earlier problem of wealth redistribution. It has become known in the economics profession as "the problem of social cost." Pigou argued that there are cases of market failure[25] in which private benefits from a particular activity impose costs on third parties. Pollution is the obvious example, although there are many others, he said. The benefits to the polluter are immediate and direct, but there is no market-produced incentive for him to cease polluting as long as his costs of operation are less than expected revenues.[26] Part of these costs are borne by someone else. At most, the polluter bears only part of the costs (stinging eyes, for example), but he reaps all of the rewards (lower production costs). He continues to pollute the environment. Total costs in the community – *social* costs – are therefore greater than the polluter's personal private costs. Followers of Pigou's analysis frequently argue that the State should redistribute this "stolen" wealth back to the original owners, perhaps through a tax on polluters and tax reductions for victims, so as to balance total social benefits (from production) and total social costs.

There is a hidden problem with this line of reasoning, one which was not discovered for almost half a century. Buchanan points to it: "The Pigouvian norm aims at bringing marginal private costs, *as these influence choice*, into line with social costs, *as*

---

25. Tyler Cowen (ed.), *The Theory of Market Failure: A Critical Examination* (Fairfax, Virginia: George Mason University Press, 1988).

26. Yes, yes, I know: "the present value of an expected future stream of income, discounted by the prevailing rate of interest." But sometimes I prefer to write in English.

these are objectively measured. Only with objective measurability can the proper corrective devices be introduced."[27] The problem is this: choice-influencing costs are exclusively subjective, according to modern economic theory. Only choice-influenced costs can be "objectively measured" (maybe). How can the judges impose objective costs that will be appropriate – scientifically appropriate – to reduce the existing level of pollution to a socially appropriate level?

This raises many other questions. How can civil judges know what is the socially appropriate level of pollution? How can they preserve the legal predictability of the courts if they cannot specify in advance the appropriate penalties? How can they be even vaguely confident that "the punishment fits the crime" of polluting? But these questions did not get asked for half a century, although they were implied by Robbins' original critique. What finally got scholars to start asking them was an essay by R. H. Coase.

Conclusion

The dilemma of modern economics is the dilemma of value theory. If economic value is exclusively subjectively determined, then it is impossible for economists as scientists to recommend socially beneficial policies. There is no valid concept of *social benefit* if all economic value is exclusively subjective. The professional realization of this truth came when Lionel Robbins challenged A. C. Pigou's defense of the graduated income tax. There is no common value scale that links the minds of individuals, Robbins said. Therefore, we cannot legitimately make scientific interpersonal comparisons of subjective utility.

Harrod understood where this argument necessarily leads, and he rejected it. So did Robbins, once Harrod challenged him. But neither of them could escape its truth. Logically, they

---

27. Buchanan, *Cost and Choice: An Inquiry in Economic Theory* (Chicago: University of Chicago Press, 1969), p. 74.

had to abandon the scientific basis of policy-making. They refused. Instead, they implicitly abandoned the scientific ideal of economics in order to save the policy-making side of the economics profession. Their legacy is universal today.

The irony is that in order to save the ideal of economic policy-making, the economists have had to abandon the epistemological foundations of modern economic science. This is not discussed in public. It is doubtful that most academically certified economists are aware of it. They go about their work as if this glaring contradiction had not been brought into the open in 1938. There is a kind of unwritten agreement within the profession: *this problem will not be discussed in public*.

This is why there is a crisis in the making, what Kuhn describes as the basis of a future revolution within the guild. But the crisis keeps getting deferred because there is no way to solve this theoretical problem without publicly abandoning the myth of neutrality which undergirds the economics profession. The myth of value-free economics was exposed by the Robbins-Harrod debate, but no one discusses this fact in public. It will probably take a revolution in epistemology launched from outside the academic guild – i.e., the rejection of the myth of neutrality – to transform the economics profession.

Meanwhile, the economics profession pays a heavy price, though this cost is not subjectively perceived. Modern economics is impaled on the horns of an inescapable epistemological dilemma, a dilemma created by the economists' assertion of the discipline's moral and theological neutrality. R. H. Coase and his followers have impaled the profession on one of these horns. In the name of policy-making by free market economists, Coase has destroyed the epistemological foundation of the Chicago School's defense of private property, just as Harrod and Robbins destroyed the epistemological defense of a truly scientific economics in the name of policy-making. This is the primary thesis of this monograph.

2

THE COASE THEOREM

If, as I have already urged, there can be no scientifically or empirically neutral system of language or concepts, then the proposed construction of alternate tests and theories must proceed from within one or another paradigm-based tradition.

Thomas Kuhn[1]

Economists today freely acknowledge that Coase's 1960 essay on social cost was one of the most important scholarly essays in the history of the economics profession.[2] Without warning, it hit both the economics profession and the world of legal theory. Coase had been the author of an important study of the firm, published a generation earlier in 1937.[3] For the next two decades, he published very little in professional scholarly journals.[4]

---

1. Thomas Kuhn, *The Structure of Scientific Revolutions* (Chicago: University of Chicago Press, 1962), p. 145.
2. R. H. Coase, "The Problem of Social Cost," *Journal of Law & Economics*, III (Oct. 1960), pp. 1-44.
3. Coase, "The Nature of the Firm," *Economica* IV (1937), pp. 386-405.
4. Coase, "Business Organization and the Accountant," *The Accountant* (Oct.-Dec. 1938), a series of a dozen brief essays written for non-economists; a shortened version is reprinted by Buchanan and Thirlby in *L.S.E. Essays on Cost*; Coase, "The Marginal Cost Controversy," *Economics*, XII (Aug. 1946). A bibliography of Coase's works appears in "On the Resignation of Ronald H. Coase," *Journal of Law & Economics*,

In 1959, he published a significant article on the Federal Communications Commision.[5] Then, like a bombshell, came his essay on social cost. It has become a standard in modern economics, still found in other scholars' footnotes two decades after its publication. (Few essays that appear in scholarly economics journals ever get cited by anyone else, and certainly not by numerous economists. After five or six years, a scholarly essay in economics, assuming it ever was noticed, is cited only half as often, except for those regarded as classics.)[6]

Richard Posner goes so far as to argue in his widely read textbook on law and economics that Coase's essay and one by Guido Calabresi[7] were instrumental in launching an entire academic discipline, law and economics,[8] "the application of the theories and empirical methods of economics to the legal system across the boards."[9] The Coase Theorem (he capitalizes it, indicating his respect for it) "established a framework for analyzing the assignment of property rights and liability in economic terms. This opened a vast field of legal doctrine to fruitful economic analysis."[10] Two scholarly journals, both published by the University of Chicago, have been heavily influenced by the Coase theorem: *The Journal of Law & Economics* and *The Journal of Legal Studies*. (This is understandable, given the fact that Coase edited the *Journal of Law & Economics* for 19

XXVI (April 1983). The bulk of his academic articles came after 1960.

5. Coase, "The Federal Communications Commission," *Journal of Law & Economics*, II (1959). This essay is reprinted in Eirik G. Furubotn and Svetozar Pejovich (eds.), *The Economics of Property Rights* (Cambridge, Massachusetts: Ballinger, 1974).

6. A. W. Coats, "The Role of Scholarly Journals in the History of Economics: An Essay," *Journal of Economic Literature*, X (1972), p. 42.

7. Guido Calabresi, "Some Thoughts on Risk Distribution and the Law of Torts," *Yale Law Journal*, vol. 70 (1961), pp. 499ff.

8. For example, A. Mitchell Polinsky, *Introduction to Law & Economics* (Boston: Little, Brown, 1983).

9. Richard A. Posner, *Economic Analysis of Law* (Boston: Little, Brown, 1986), p. 19. But see also "The Fire of Truth: A Remembrance of Law and Economics at Chicago, 1932-1970," *Journal of Law & Economics*, XXVI (April 1983).

10. *Ibid.*, p. 20.

years, 1965-1983, and the *Journal of Legal Studies* is a sister publication.)[11] As Posner wrote in 1981, "Until recently, then, utilitarianism held sway in legal theory, but overt economic analysis was rare. The position is now reversed."[12] (Problem: Has economic analysis escaped the ethics of utilitarianism?)

Coase's essay was perhaps the key one in the revival of interest in the question of pollution and economics, as well as a crucially important contribution to a free market theory of property rights. And, let me say from the outset, it is a dangerously flawed essay. Few economists have seen its flaws. The first professional economist I ever heard even mention a really critical comment against it – essentially, the same criticism I had also come up with – could not get it published in a conventional professional economics journal, and he had to wait three years after he discussed his criticism with me before he saw it in print.[13]

Coase vs. Pigou

It is interesting that Coase, like Robbins in 1932, began his discussion by attacking A. C. Pigou. Coase summarized the state of the debate – it had long ceased to be debated very much – as of 1960. Pigou's statement of the problem had given the problem of social cost its traditional framework. This discussion was categorized under the general rubric of "externalities." The term refers to the imposition of a firm's costs of operation on those who are not owners of the stream of income generated by

---

11. For a survey of this literature, see the footnotes in the article by Elizabeth Hoffman and Matthew Spitzer, "The Coase Theorem: Some Experimental Tests," *Journal of Law & Economics*, XXV (April 1982), pp. 73-98. The rigor of the limiting assumptions made by the authors of this article is much greater than Coase's own formulation; the article is also far less readable or usable.

12. Richard A. Posner, *The Economics of Justice* (Cambridge, Massachusetts: Harvard University Press, 1983), p. 51.

13. Walter Block, "Coase and Demsetz on Private Property Rights," *Journal of Libertarian Studies*, I, No. 2 (1977), pp. 111-15. Dr. Block is presently a professor at Holy Cross College.

the production process. In other words, these victims are *external* to the firm or production unit, but not external to its costs of operation. Almost without exception, previous economists' discussion of externalities had ended with a consideration of what government measures are appropriate to reduce or eliminate these externalities. The conclusions reached by most economists, based on Pigou's analysis in *The Economics of Welfare* (4th ed., 1932; originally published in 1920), were as follows, Coase summarized: the producer of pollution (smoke, noise, etc.) should (1) pay damages to those injured, or (2) have a tax imposed on his production by the civil government, or (3) have his factory excluded from residential districts.[14] Coase's article broke with this tradition.

Aaron Levine summarizes Coase's breakthrough: "Assuming zero transaction costs and economic rationality, Coase, in his seminal work, demonstrated that the market mechanism is capable of eliminating negative externalities without the necessity of governmentally imposed liability rules."[15] Furthermore, the theorem leads to the conclusion that "if transactions are costless, the initial assignment of a property right will not determine the ultimate use of the property."[16] Free market economists of the Chicago School have increasingly sided with Coase. (What is also remarkable is that traditional Jewish law had adopted the basic features of the Coase theorem many centuries earlier; English law had not.[17] Why remarkable? Because Exodus 22:5-6 is clearly on Pigou's side.[18])

---

14. Coase, "Social Cost," p. 1.
15. Aaron Levine, *Free Enterprise and Jewish Law: Aspects of Jewish Business Ethics* (New York: Ktav Publishing House, Yeshiva University Press, 1980), p. 59.
16. Posner, *Economic Analysis of Law*, p. 7.
17. Yehoshua Liebermann, "The Coase Theorem in Jewish Law," *Journal of Legal Studies*, X (June 1981), pp. 293-303.
18. Gary North, *Tools of Dominion: The Case Laws of Exodus* (Tyler, Texas: Institute for Christian Economics, 1990), ch. 18.

The problem is, of course, that *there are and always will be transaction costs*.[19] Or, I should say, this is *a* problem. The major problem is that his theorem assigns zero economic value – and therefore zero relevance – to the sense of moral and legal right associated with a willful violation of private ownership. It ignores the economic relevance of the public's sense of moral outrage when there is no enforcement by the civil government of owners' legal immunities from invasion, even if this invasion is done in the name of some "more efficient" social good or social goal. This is why I conclude that the Coase theorem is one of the most morally insidious pieces of academic nonsense ever to hit the economics profession; worse, it has infected the thinking of a generation of very bright and very glib free market economists and legal theorists. Coase has served as the Typhoid Mary of Chicago School economics for three decades. His essay drastically compromised the academic case for liberty. It has imposed private costs on those of us who are attempting to make a case for free market economics. In this sense, Coase's theorem is an example of *externalities*: net private benefits for Coase and net social costs for the economics profession and any society whose courts adopt his approach. The victims cannot sue him in civil court. The best we can do is offer a pollution-abatement system: proof that his whole argument is specious.

Coase fully recognized from the beginning the nature of the technical economic problem he had raised, namely, *the impossibility of a world in which there are no transaction costs*. (The moral issues related to property rights he does not even discuss as relevant in some way to economic analysis, as we shall see.) Therefore, he allows civil judges to intervene to settle disputes. But there is a problem here: Coase cannot escape that nagging problem ignored by Pigou and all welfare economists, namely,

---

19. For a brief introduction to the question of transaction costs, see Oliver E. Williamson, "Transaction-Cost Economics: The Governance of Contractual Relations," *Journal of Law & Economics*, XXII (Oct. 1979), pp. 233-61.

the problem of interpersonal comparisons of subjective utility. Coase's "scientific" case against Pigou rests on the implicit assertion that men, especially judges, can make such comparisons in their act of formulating social policy. The only professional response deeply critical of Coase has been made by Austrian School economists, who recognize the weakness of the Chicago School's presuppositions concerning interpersonal comparisons of subjective utility. Still, their criticism leaves much to be desired, for if taken seriously, it would become impossible to defend the idea of government penalties against polluters.

The Ethical Pea Beneath the Neutral Shell

The astounding fact about the Coase theorem is that every economist knows that there are no cases of exchanges in which there are zero transaction costs. They also know that the Coase theorem applies *only* where there are zero transaction costs. Yet they do not identify the Coase theorem as an instance of curious but utterly irrelevant academic speculation. Instead, they try to work with his theorem. Richard Posner, an economist and a judge in the U.S. Appeals Court (Seventh Circuit), admits that the Coase theorem applies only to zero transaction cost situations, yet he has devoted much of his academic career to pursuing the economic implications of the Coase theorem in the field of law. He knows that Coase's initial assumption – that transaction costs are zero – cannot be true in the real world. Posner writes:

> The economist does not merely decree that absolute rights [of ownership – G.N.] be created and then fall silent as to where they should be vested. To be sure, if market transactions were costless, the economist would not care where a right was initially vested. The process of voluntary exchange would costlessly reallocate it to whoever valued it the most. But once the unrealistic assumption of zero transaction costs is abandoned, the assignment of rights becomes determinate. If transaction costs are

positive (though presumably low, for otherwise it would be inefficient to create an absolute right), the wealth-maximization principle requires the initial vesting of rights in those who are likely to value them most, so as to minimize transaction costs. This is the economic reason for giving a worker the right to sell his labor and a woman the right to determine her sexual partners. If assigned randomly to strangers, these rights would generally (not invariably) be repurchased by the worker and the woman; the costs of the rectifying transaction can be avoided if the right is assigned at the outset to the user who values it most.[20]

Posner openly admits that in some cases, even where transaction costs are low, the worker or the woman in his example would not (i.e., could not afford to) repurchase these rights of ownership. This follows from his definition of value: "The most important thing to bear in mind about the concept of value is that it is based on what people are willing to pay for something rather than on the happiness they would derive from having it. . . . The individual who would like very much to have some good but is unwilling or unable to pay anything for it – perhaps because he is destitute – does not value the good in the sense in which I am using the term 'value.' "[21]

The conclusion is obvious, and he does not hesitate to draw it: "Equivalently, the wealth of society is the aggregate satisfaction of those preferences (the only ones that have ethical weight in a system of wealth maximization) that are backed up by money, that is, that are registered in a market." In short, people's demonstrated preferences – money on the line – are the only ones that possess "ethical weight" in his definition of wealth-maximization. Does this include marriage? Of course. Does this include games of chance? Of course. "Much of eco-

---

20. Posner, *Economics of Justice*, p. 71. For a critique of Posner's approach to the law, see Buchanan, "Good Economics – Bad Law," *Virginia Law Review*, LX (1974), pp. 483-92. See also the biting and incisive essay by Arthur Allen Leff, "Economic Analysis of Law: Some Realism About Nominalism," *ibid.*, pp. 451-82.

21. Posner, *ibid.*, pp. 60, 61.

nomic life is still organized on barter principles. The 'marriage market,' child rearing, and a friendly game of bridge are examples. These services have value which could be monetized by reference to substitute services sold in explicit markets or in other ways."[22]

Question: Who should make the initial distribution of an ownership right to whomever "values it the most"? How does this sovereign agent know scientifically which potential owners "are likely to value them [ownership rights] the most"? In short: *By what standard of value does he make the initial distribution?* Dead silence from Chicago School economists. To say anything at this point would be a public admission that economic science is no longer regarded by them as being value-free. The Coase theorem would have to be acknowledged for what it is: an important component in a giant academic shell game. The ethical pea is always concealed beneath the seemingly neutral scientific shell of cost-benefit analysis. To paraphrase the late John Mitchell, U.S. Attorney General under President Nixon: "Watch what the economist does, not what he says he is doing." He is invariably making interpersonal comparisons of subjective utility every time he recommends a policy decision.

The debate over social costs raises once again the ancient debate between objective and subjective knowledge. It is one of the persistent antinomies in all humanist thought. The epistemological problem of social cost is an *ethical* problem, and as such, humanists cannot solve it "scientifically."

Reciprocal Harm

Coase reformulated the terms of the debate over externalities. "The question is commonly thought of as one in which A inflicts harm on B and what has been decided is: how should we restrain A? But this is wrong. We are dealing with a problem of a reciprocal nature. To avoid the harm to B would

---

22. *Ibid.*, p. 61.

inflict harm on A. The real question that has to be decided is: should A be allowed to harm B or should B be allowed to harm A? The problem is to avoid the more serious harm."[23]

Such reasoning is ethically perverse, if accepted as a methodological standard governing economic analysis in all instances involving economic action. It would be just as easy to say of kidnapping that any restrictions on kidnapping by the State harm the kidnapper, and that a lack of restrictions harms the victims. If we are going to build an economic system in terms of the supposedly "reciprocal nature of harm" – that each economic actor suffers harm when he is restricted from acting according to his immediate whim – then economics becomes positively wicked, not value-free, in its attempt to sort out just how much harm the courts will allow each party to impose on the other.

There are some areas of life – areas governed by biblical morality – in which such "cost-benefit analyses" must not even be contemplated. For example, any attempt to impose cost-benefit analyses on competing techniques of mass genocide, including abortion, is demonic, not scientifically neutral. Whether a genocidal society should adopt either gas chambers or lethal injections for adults, or either saline solutions or suction devices for unborn infants, cannot be solved in terms of comparative rates of cost-efficiency, for the economist always ignores a major "exogenous variable": the wrath of God. God will efficiently judge those individuals who promote all such cost-efficient systems, as well as societies that adopt them. If legal restrictions against mass genocide harm the potential mass murderers and the purchaser of their services, this is all to the good. Society faces no "reduction in social benefits" whatsoever. Justice does cost something, but the net economic effect is positive, whether the economist sees this or not. There is no reduction in net social benefits as a result of the thwarted goals

---

23. Coase, "Social Cost," p. 2.

of the now-restricted (or previously executed) genocidal technocrats. Yet we live in a society in which the right to life has been successfully challenged in the courts (including church courts) in the name of personal and social costs. Should we be surprised that R. H. Coase's essay won him the Nobel Prize?

Coase offered the following example of reciprocal harm. What about cattle that stray onto another man's property and destroy crops? This, it should be noted, is precisely the issue dealt with by Exodus 22:5: "If a man shall cause a field or vineyard to be eaten, and shall put in his beast, and shall feed in another man's field; of the best of his own field, and of the best of his own vineyard, shall he make restitution." Coase writes: "If it is inevitable that some cattle will stray, an increase in the supply of meat can only be obtained at the expense of a decrease in the supply of crops. The nature of the choice is clear: meat or crops?"[24]

This appears to be correct economic analysis, as far as it goes. It forces us to think about the problem in terms of what members of the society must give up, meat vs. crops. But his next sentence is the very heart of the problem, and he never shows how economists – or anyone else, for that matter – can, as scientists, make an economically rational (i.e., value-neutral) choice in the name of society: crops vs. meat. Indeed, humanistic economics cannot possibly answer this question because of the inability of economists, as scientists, to make interpersonal comparisons of subjective utility.[25] But the economics profession refuses to acknowledge the existence of this dilemma.

---

24. *Idem.*

25. In other words, we cannot make scientific comparisons of the utility gained by one person vs. the utility thereby forfeited by another man. There is no unit of "utility measurement" which is common to both men. We cannot as neutral scientists legitimately say that one man has gained greater utility (a subjective evaluation on his part) than another man has lost (another subjective evaluation). I discuss this problem in *The Dominion Covenant: Genesis* (2nd ed.; Tyler, Texas: Institute for Christian Economics, 1987), ch. 4.

Subjective Value vs. Social Policy

Coase never comes to grips with this problem. "What answer should be given is, of course, not clear until we know the value of what is obtained as well as the value of what is sacrificed to attain it."[26] *Value?* As economists, we need to ask ourselves several questions: Value to whom? Society as a whole? The value to the cattle owner? The value to the farmer? Also, how can judges make such estimates of economic value, since all economic value is supposedly exclusively subjective? Questions of economic value are the main problems raised by his paper, yet he cannot answer them by means of the "scientific economics" he proclaims. No economist can. Economist Peter Lewin has gone to the heart of the matter when he writes in a withering critique of Coase that

> costs are individual and private and cannot be "social." The social-cost concept requires the summation of individual costs, which is impossible if costs are seen in utility terms. The notion of social cost as reflected by market prices (or even more problematically by hypothetical prices in the absence of a market for the item) has validity only in conditions so far removed from reality as to make its use as a general tool of policy analysis highly suspect. . . .
>
> The foregoing suggests that any perception of efficiency at the social level is illusory. And the essential thread in all the objections to the efficiency concept, be it wealth effects, distortions, or technological changes, is the refusal by economists to make interpersonal comparisons of utility. Social cost falls to the ground precisely because individual evaluations of the sacrifice involved in choosing among options cannot be compared.[27]

---

26. Coase, "Social Cost," p. 2.
27. Peter Lewin, "Pollution Externalities: Social Cost and Strict Liability," *Cato Journal*, II (Spring 1982), pp. 220, 222.

The inability of anyone to make scientifically valid interpersonal comparisons of subjective utility has once again smashed all the hopes of the free market's humanist defenders to deal scientifically (i.e., without any appeal to either civil justice or morality) with a problem of social policy. The more astute "anarcho-capitalists" have understood this, and have thereby abandoned the very idea of social utility and social costs. They have also abandoned the idea of civil government.[28] But they have not been able to demonstrate how people can deal successfully with the problems created by such technological developments as the internal combustion engine. But at least they are consistent. They do not search for "fools' gold" intellectual solutions to "scientifically" insoluble problems. They do not search for pseudo-market solutions – "What would the correct market price be in the absence of a market?" – or solutions involving the hypothetical (and scientifically impossible) ability of judges to make scientifically valid social cost-benefit analyses in settling disputes. *There can be no scientifically valid answers to such social problems, given the presuppositions of modern, subjectivistic, individualistic economic theory.* Yet the approach used by Coase and his academic followers to deal with these questions assumes that there *are* scientifically valid answers to them.

Conclusion

Since there are no "neutral, scientific" answers, Coase's whole essay is an exercise in intellectual gymnastics – an illusion of scientific precision.[29] Nevertheless, it is considered a classic

---

28. "There is no government solution to pollution or to the common-pool problem because government is the problem." Gerald P. O'Driscoll, Jr., "Pollution, Libertarianism, and the Law," *ibid.*, p. 50.

29. This same illusion of scientific precision is at the heart of virtually every professional journal in economics, every mathematical equation, and every call for scientific policy-making issued by members of the economists' guild. The day an economist admits to himself that no economist can make interpersonal comparisons of subjective utility is the day that his public claims of economics' objective, scientific precision make him a charlatan. The day before, he was simply ignorant.

essay, a pioneering work which literally created a new approach in both economics and legal theory. What is revealing is that the economics profession as a whole has refused to face up to this problem, and it took over two decades for a critical analysis based on a 1938 observation by Lionel Robbins to be applied to the Coase theorem by Peter Lewin, who was (1) an assistant professor (untenured) at (2) an obscure university to be published in (3) a new intellectual journal that has no following within the academic community.[30] Such is academia.[31]

---

30. In my 1973 book, *An Introduction to Christian Economics*, I briefly referred to "R. H. Coase's clever sophistry," (p. 94n), but did not have space to pursue his arguments in detail. Some readers may think I should have let it go at that.

31. Lewin presently works for a computer software firm.

3

COASE VS. PROPERTY RIGHTS

Anomaly appears only against the background provided by the paradigm. The more precise and far-reaching that paradigm is, the more sensitive an indicator it provides of anomaly and hence of an occasion for paradigm change. . . . By ensuring that the paradigm will not be too easily surrendered, resistance guarantees that scientists will not be lightly distracted and that the anomalies that lead to paradigm change will penetrate existing knowledge to the core.

Thomas Kuhn[1]

We come now to the issue of property rights. The meaning of "property rights" is this: individuals or associations represented by individuals possess a legal right to prevent others from stealing, invading, destroying, or otherwise interfering with their property. Owners therefore possess a legal right *to exclude others* from the use of specified property. This is analogous to covenantal forms of exclusion: the State's right to exclude non-citizens from voting; the married person's right to exclude others from sexual access to the partner; and the church's right to exclude non-members or non-Christians from

---

1. Thomas Kuhn, *The Structure of Scientific Revolutions* (Chicago: University of Chicago Press, 1962), p. 65.

the communion table. The phrase "property rights" means that there is a legally enforceable "bundle of rights" that is associated with specific forms of property.

Coase's essay undermines the very concept of private property rights. He offers a detailed, carefully constructed argument concerning the marginal gains to the cattleman vs. the marginal losses to the farmer from a roaming steer. What the essay demonstrates, *assuming that the psychological costs to the farmer of the cattleman's violation of his property rights are never taken into consideration*, is this: excluding transaction costs and information costs,[2] as well as assuming perfect competition (omniscience), *the gain or loss to society is the same*, whether the cattleman compensates the farmer for the value of the lost crops, should the cattle be left to roam, or the farmer compensates the cattleman for the higher costs of meat production, if the cattle are kept away from the farmer's crops (higher feed costs, costs of fencing, etc.). Again, assuming "conditions of perfect competition," Coase concludes: "Whether the cattle-raiser pays the farmer to leave the land uncultivated or himself rents the land by paying the land-owner an amount slightly greater than the farmer would pay (if the farmer was himself renting the land), the final result would be the same and would maximize the value of production."[3]

Given his initial, unrealistic hypothetical assumptions about free goods – transaction costs, information costs, and perfect competition – this conclusion initially appears to be correct, *assuming that farmers have no commitment to a sense of justice concerning property rights*. It also assumes that *members of such a society do not and will not suffer any additional economic losses when the civil government refuses to make cattle owners responsible for the damage their animals cause*. In other words, it assumes that when civil

---

2. ". . . when the damaging business has to pay for all damage caused *and* the pricing system works smoothly (strictly this means that the operation of the pricing system is without cost)." Coase, "Social Cost," p. 2.

3. *Ibid.*, p. 6.

judges use Coase's theorem as a standard of judgment and a legal precedent, property owners will experience no loss. Both assumptions are implicit to Coase's thesis, and both are categorically incorrect. Coase begins with an unreal world in which transaction costs are defined away, and from this he draws his equally unrealistic conclusions.[4]

I say that his conclusion *initially* appears to be correct – that in a zero-cost world, the outcome of the bargaining process would be the same, the value of cattle vs. the value of crops. Yet in a perceptive essay by Donald Regan, we learn that Coase has no warrant for making this conclusion. Coase assumes that the free market's voluntaristic bargaining process will produce the same economic results that a compulsory civil court's decision would produce if it were to follow Coase's concept of net social cost, but why should we believe this? Regan says that Coase offers no model of how this bargaining process would inevitably produce such identical results *in the absence of specified and legally enforceable property rights*. For example, sometimes a bargainer makes economic threats of non-cooperation that must be occasionally enforced in order to persuade the other party that he should take such threats seriously, even if the actual carrying out of the threat may injure the threat-maker in the short run. How does Coase know what the short-run or long-run outcome of a bargaining process will be? He doesn't.[5] This is simply another way of saying that we cannot confidently

---

4. Writes Jules L. Coleman: "No term in the philosopher's lexicon is more imprecisely defined than is the economist's term 'transaction costs.' Almost anything counts as a transaction cost. But if we are to count the failure to reach agreement on the division of surplus as necessarily resulting from transaction costs (I have no doubt that sometimes it does), then by 'transaction cost' we must mean literally anything that threatens the efficiency of market exchange. In that case, it could hardly come as a surprise that, in the absence of transaction costs so conceived, market exchange is efficient." Coleman, "Economics and the Law: A Critical Review of the Foundations of the Economic Approach to Law," *Ethics*, 94 (July 1984), p. 666.

5. Donald H. Regan, "The Problem of Social Cost Revisited," *Journal of Law & Economics*, XV (Oct. 1972), pp. 428-32.

make social and economic evaluations of real-world events by abstracting economic theory from temporal reality – i.e., by creating a mental world in which there are no costs, no ignorance of present or future opportunities, and no need of threats to achieve our goals.

Coase states clearly what he thinks the economic problem is. "The economic problem in all cases of harmful effects is how to maximize the value of production."[6] Furthermore, he is no fool. Later in the essay, he drops his essay's initial assumption of zero transaction costs, perfect competition, and zero information costs.[7] Of course, in real life there are transaction costs to settle disputes. For this reason, there is a role for civil government in settling costly disputes.[8] "All solutions have costs," including solutions imposed by the civil government.[9]

One underlying presupposition distorts all of Coase's analysis – a presupposition which is all too common (and unstated) in Chicago School economic analysis: the legitimacy of leaving aside issues of right and wrong, of justice, of *equity*. Coase writes: "Of course, if market transactions were costless, all that matters (questions of equity apart) is that the rights of the various parties should be well-defined and the results of legal actions easy to forecast."[10] Problem: How can we discuss "the rights of the various parties" if we leave aside questions of

---

6. Coase, "Social Cost," p. 15.

7. There is always the nagging suspicion that once these formal theoretical assumptions are dropped, the whole intellectual performance becomes nothing more than a scholarly puzzle game. Will any of the conclusions concerning the world of the theoretical model still remain accurate, let alone applicable, once we begin to discuss the empirical world? And how can we know for sure? Only through intuition – a nonrational, nonlogical category. See Gary North, "Economics: From Reason to Intuition," in Gary North (ed.), *Foundations of Christian Scholarship: Essays in the Van Til Perspective* (Vallecito, California: Ross House, 1976.) See also North, *Dominion Covenant: Genesis* (2nd. ed.; Tyler, Texas: Institute for Christian Economics, 1987), pp. 350-53.

8. Coase, "Social Cost," pp. 15-19.

9. *Ibid.*, p. 18.

10. *Ibid.*, p. 19.

equity – questions of right and wrong? In short, how can we discuss "rights" apart from discussing what is morally right?

This is the problem that the economics profession has faced from the beginning. Coase's essay denies the relevance of the question. That is the problem with Coase's essay.

Discounting Moral Outrage to Zero

Questions of equity apart: here is a continuing assumption in the "value-free, morally neutral" economic hypotheses of modern free market economists. They apparently think that questions of equity, being questions of opinion and morality, cannot be dealt with scientifically, nor can economists, as scientists, put a price tag on violations of moral principle. They conveniently ignore the inescapable conclusion of subjectivist economics and methodological individualism, namely, that *there is no scientific way to measure costs and benefits of any kind*, since interpersonal comparisons of subjective utility are impossible for mortals to make. Economists naively believe that there is a neutral, value-free science of economics, but not of morality.

They are correct about the impossibility of neutral morality; they are incorrect about the existence of a value-free economics. Economics deals with value, and there is no value-free value. The moment an economist raises the question of value – social value, personal value, value of Gross National Product – he has left the hypothetical world of value-free science. Such a world is mythical anyway. But economists have invested so much of their intellectual and professional capital in this myth for so long that they find it difficult to abandon it. If they were to abandon this myth, their peers would not take them seriously, and they would not get their unreadable and unread essays into professional journals any more.

One of Coase's academic defenders, Yale Law School's Guido Calabresi, carries the Coase theorem to distant shores of speculation and social unreality. He says that the Coase theorem demonstrates that "the same allocation of resources will come about regardless of which of two joint cost causers is initially charged with the cost, in other words, regardless of liability rules."[11] He repeats Coase's example of the smoke-producing factory that damages the wheat crop of local farmers. "For example, if we assume that the cost of factory smoke which destroys neighboring farmers' wheat can be avoided more cheaply by a smoke control device than by growing a smoke resistant wheat, then, even if the loss is left on the farmers they will, under the assumptions made, pay the factory to install the smoke control device. This would, in the short run, result in more factories relative to farmers and lower relative farm output than if the liability rule had been reversed. But if, as a result of this liability rule, farm output is too low relative to factory output those who lose from this 'misallocation' would have every reason to bribe farmers to produce more and factories to produce less. The process would continue until no bargain could improve the allocation of resources."[12]

A Response to Calabresi

It sounds so precise, so logical. It also sounds crazy. Here is why it really is crazy. *First*, there are always transaction costs in life. To begin with any other assumption is to begin with utopianism. It makes as much sense as beginning with the assumption of the omniscience of the participants in exchange, which is another familiar assumption in almost all modern economic thought, especially in the journals. Without this theoretical ideal of omniscience, economic theory would have no formulas and equations, but professional economists would rather die than give up their formulas and equations. The epistemological problem is this: once the theoretical model is formulated in terms of a hypothetical set of assumptions that cannot exist in

---

11. Guido Calabresi, "Transaction Costs, Resource Allocation and Liability Rules – A Comment," *Journal of Law & Economics*, XI (April 1968), p. 67.

12. *Ibid.*, pp. 67-68.

the real world, it takes an act of will for the economist to bring the model to bear on real-world problems without importing radical utopianism into his analysis. The debate over the Coase theorem is a Nobel Prize-winning example of an unsuccessful attempt by an economist to discard an economic model's totally utopian initial assumptions, yet still retain the model's conclusions for analytic purposes.[13] That it should be taken seriously by so many economists is evidence of the theoretical bankruptcy of modern economics. That legal theorists should also take it seriously is frightening.

Second, the allocation problem and its solutions are not primarily technical and empirical problems but rather ethical and epistemological. Calabresi poses the problem, and then answers it (as Chicago School economists usually do) in terms of the least costly solution technically, not in terms of any visible ethical principle. "The primary implication is that problems of misallocation of resources and externalities are not theoretical but empirical ones. The resource allocation aim is to approximate, both closely and cheaply, the result the market would bring about if bargaining actually were costless."[14] In other words, the civil judge is to pretend that he can approximate the

---

13. Calabresi writes: "Thus, if one assumes rationality, no transaction costs, and no legal impediments to bargaining, *all* misallocations of resources would be fully cured in the market by bargains. Far from being surprising, this statement is tautological, at least if one accepts any of the various classic definitions of misallocation. These ultimately come down to a statement akin to the following: A misallocation exists when there is available a possible reallocation in which all those who would lose from the reallocation could be fully compensated by those who would gain, and, at the end of this compensation process, there would still be some who would be better off than before." *Ibid.*, p. 68. This is one more application of Pareto's optimality theorem, perhaps the most non-optimal and misleading idea ever to get into the literature of economics. It is conceptually a dead end; it is also quite popular. I agree with Lutz and Lux: if it were buried forever, we could place a tombstone over it bearing these words: "Everybody has been made better off and nobody worse off." Mark A. Lutz and Kenneth Lux, *The Challenge of Humanistic Economics* (Menlo Park, California: Benjamin/Cummings, 1979), p. 101. Chapter 5 of their book is delightful: "The New Welfare Economics: Value-Free or Value-Less?"

14. Calabresi, *ibid.*, p. 69.

allocation that a free market would produce, if free markets were costless. This, it should be mentioned, is a denial of the most important of all theorems in economics: scarcity. A civil judge capable of completing this assigned task would be a scarce resource indeed! Of course, he would possess this advantage: since the initial limiting condition is impossible – zero transaction costs – nobody can produce a model that will prove that his allocation is off the mark, economically speaking. He is therefore free to decide the case on the basis of net social cost, and nobody can say for sure that his estimate is incorrect.

How would this utopian task best be accomplished? Calabresi combines the false precision of the economist with the real obfuscation of the lawyer to produce this problematical conclusion: "This question depends in large part on the relative *cost* of reaching the correct result by each of these means (an empirical problem which probably could be resolved, at least approximately, in most instances), and the relative *chances* of reaching a widely *wrong* result depending on the method used (also an empirical problem but one as to which it is hard to get other than 'guess' type data). The resolution of these two problems and their interplay is *the* problem of accomplishing optimal resource allocations."[15] Some problem!

So, the allocation problem for welfare economics is merely an empirical problem. But this so-called empirical problem cannot be solved scientifically, logically, or technically, for there is no way for the scientific economist to deal with the key epistemological problem: the impossibility of making scientific interpersonal comparisons of subjective utility. Yet the Chicago School economists babble on in their journals as if more precise measurements could somehow solve what they admit is *the* allocation problem. It is as if a gunnery sergeant were attempting to hit a target at the edge of the universe by adding just a bit more gunpowder to the load. It is simply a technical prob-

---

15. *Idem.*

lem, you understand. It is as if a sprinter were trying to reduce his time in the hundred meter race to one second flat by shaving a tenth of a second off his time in each preliminary heat. It is an empirical problem, you understand. If he could just get better shoes or a track with better traction!

Calabresi knows all this. He acknowledges that the decision which would be reached if the transactions were costless is an "unreachable goal."[16] He also acknowledges that "the gains which reaching nearer the goal would bring are not usually subject to precise definition or quantification. They are, in fact, largely defined by guesses. As a result, the question of whether a given law is worth its costs (in terms of better resource allocation) is rarely susceptible to empirical proof. . . . It is precisely the province of good government to make guesses as to what laws are likely to be worth their costs. Hopefully it will use what empirical information is available and seek to develop empirical information which is not currently available (how much information is worth *its* costs is also a question, however). But there is no reason to assume that in the absence of conclusive information no government action is better than some action."[17]

Please get his argument clear in your mind: welfare economics is essentially an empirical science, except that empiricism cannot really solve the issues of welfare economics, so the State will have to decide what is the appropriate allocation of resources, but economists nevertheless hope that the bureaucrats will use empiricism as the means of finding solutions to the specific allocation problems, though only an economically efficient quantity and quality of empiricism should be purchased. In any case, the State's decision will necessarily be based primarily on guesswork. If this explanation resembles a walk through a hall of mirrors, it is because it *is* a hall of mirrors. Yet virtually all essays in welfare economics are little more than

---

16. *Idem.*
17. *Ibid.*, pp. 69-70.

guided tours into (but never out of) this conceptual hall of mirrors.

The allocation problem of welfare economics cannot be solved by humanist economics, for the economists are overcome by a series of antinomies: the subjective-objective dualism, the individual-society dualism, the problem of fixed law and the endless flux of circumstances, and the overwhelming and unanswered problem of interpersonal comparisons of subjective utility. It is all premised on this formula: *dialectics plus intuition equals cost-effective justice*. This formula does not produce anything except additional scholarly articles for professors' vitae – in short, negative social returns.

Third, and far more important for social analysis, there would be a sense of outrage among the victims of the polluting factory if there were no State-enforced liability rules. The initial reaction of any one of the victims, if he knows that the civil law does not protect his ownership rights automatically, may be to blow up the factory or murder its owner. The multiplication of acts of violence would be assured under such a non-liability legal order. *The issue of economic efficiency therefore cannot be separated from the issue of judicial equity.* This is what Chicago School economists and legal theorists never show any signs of having understood. When righteous men are thwarted in their cause by seekers of local "efficiency" who care nothing about the ethics of the solution, there will be serious social consequences. To discuss the efficiency of any given transaction without also discussing the equity of it is to begin to deliver the society into the hands of socialist revolutionaries. Or, to put it in language more familiar to Chicago School economists, *penalizing righteousness in the name of economic efficiency is not a zero-cost decision*. Any approach to economics that ignores righteousness and justice as valid economic factors is a trip into the hall of mirrors. Yet this is almost universally the assumption of all schools of modern economics.

Micro-Efficiency and Macro-Revolution

It is not possible to discover an economically efficient solution to just one transaction. We cannot be efficient in just one thing. The question of efficiency is not simply a microeconomic issue; it is also macroeconomic. We cannot discover an efficient solution to any economic problem that does not in some way affect the whole social order. In short, *we cannot do just one thing efficiently*. We need to heed the warning of biologist Garrett Hardin: "The dream of the philosopher's stone is old and well known, and has its counterparts in the ideas of skeleton keys and panaceas. . . . We now look askance at any one who sets out to find a philosopher's stone. The mythology of our time is built more around the reciprocal dream – the dream of a highly specific agent *which will do only one thing*. . . . The moral of the myth can be put in various ways. One: Wishing won't make it so. Two: Every change has its price. Three (and this one I like best): *We can never do merely one thing*."[18]

The system of justice that governs any social order is itself a net producer or reducer of both macro-efficiency and micro-efficiency. *Equity can never be segregated from efficiency*. If our judges' supposedly economically efficient decisions at the micro level call into question the moral integrity of the prevailing legal order, we have not yet reached an efficient solution to our microeconomic problem. This is why it is astonishing to find economist and Talmudist Aaron Levine siding with Coase: "While the principle of equity is promoted by the selection of appropriate liability rules, economic efficiency is realized when the negative externality is eliminated by the *least-cost* method. Hence, should it be less costly to avoid crop damage by growing smoke-resistant wheat than by installing a smoke-control device, the former method should be adopted. Whether the farmer or

---

18. Garrett Hardin, "The Cybernetics of Competition: A Biologist's View of Society," in Helmut Schoeck and James W. Wiggins (eds.), *Central Planning and Mercantilism* (Princeton, New Jersey: Van Nostrand, 1964), p. 84.

the factory-owner should bear the additional expense of eliminating the negative externality is entirely irrelevant as far as the efficiency question is concerned."[19] Charge the farmers for the cost of the factory's smoke abatement, and you have violated the principle of justice that governs Exodus 22:5-6. There will eventually be negative repercussions, whether economists believe in God or not.

Conclusion

By means of a logically rigorous intellectual defense of the free market's process of allocating access to property, R. H. Coase has presented a case against the necessity of the State's imposing restraints on those who initiate acts that inflict damage on other people. While his discussion centers on damage to property, the legal issue is not the rights of property, but rather the legal right of an individual to exclude others from using his property. I wish Coase would write an article on marriage vows and adultery in terms of the ethical and legal standards he sets forth in "The Problem of Social Cost." He should also add an appendix on rape.

Certified economists are all too often certifiable idiots. They are revolutionaries who toss equations rather than bombs. The reductionism of economic logic, even without the equations, has become so great that it has just about eliminated the real-world relevance of the academic discipline of economics, especially its academic journals. That which is obvious escapes these people. They speak of a world of zero transaction costs and zero rules establishing legal liability as if it would not be a world of turmoil, unpredictability, and violence. It is the establishment of liability rules that makes civil order possible. Social order is clearly too important a matter to be left in the hands of economists, even technically rigorous Chicago School economists.

---

19. Aaron Levine, *Free Enterprise and Jewish Law: Aspects of Jewish Business Ethics* (New York: Ktav Publishing House, Yeshiva University Press, 1980), p. 59.

4

ROTHBARD'S CHALLENGE TO COASE

Often a new paradigm emerges, at least in embryo, before a crisis has developed far or has been explicitly recognized.

Thomas Kuhn[1]

One economist who has seen at least some of the implications of Coase's position is Murray Rothbard. Rothbard very early recognized the truth of Robbins' refutation of Pigou, namely, that there can be no scientifically valid interpersonal comparisons of subjective utility.[2] He has written a critique of the Coase theorem which underscores some of the points I raised in the original draft of this study before I discovered Rothbard's 1982 essay. But he goes to the full logical conclusion of the subjectivist school, namely, that *there can be no such thing as social cost* – not simply that economists cannot measure it, but that it does not exist as a category of economics.[3] He discusses

---

1. Thomas Kuhn, *The Structure of Scientific Revolutions* (Chicago: University of Chicago Press, 1962), p. 86.

2. Murray N. Rothbard, "Toward a Reconstruction of Utility and Welfare Economics," in Mary Sennholz (ed.), *On Freedom and Free Enterprise: Essays in Honor of Ludwig von Mises* (Princeton, New Jersey: Van Nostrand, 1956). This has been reprinted by Liberty Press, Indianapolis, Indiana.

3. The Christian economist must reject this thesis. There are indeed social costs

the case of the farmer whose orchard is burned by sparks emitted by a passing train. His analysis focuses on the farmer's subjective costs that are imposed by the railroad's aggression. Should the State solve this dispute by forcing the railroad to pay the farmer the market value of the lost trees?

> There are many problems with this [Coase's] theory. First, income and wealth are important *to the parties involved*, although they might not be to uninvolved economists. It makes a great deal of difference to both of them who has to pay whom. Second, this thesis works only if we deliberately ignore psychological factors. Costs are not only monetary. The farmer might well have an attachment to the orchard far beyond the monetary damage. Therefore, the orchard might be worth far more to him than the $100,000 in damages. . . .
>
> The love of the farmer for his orchard is part of a larger difficulty for the Coase-Demsetz doctrine: Costs are purely subjective and not measurable in monetary terms. Coase and Demsetz have a proviso in their indifference thesis that all "transaction costs" be zero. If they are not, then they advocate allocating the property rights to whichever route entails minimum social transaction costs. But once we understand that costs are subjective to each individual and therefore unmeasurable, we see that costs cannot be added up. But if all costs, including transaction costs, cannot be added, then there is no such thing as "social transaction costs," and they cannot be compared. . . .
>
> Another serious problem with the Coase-Demsetz approach is that pretending to be value-free, they in reality import the ethical norm of "efficiency," and assert that property rights should be assigned on the basis of such efficiency. But even if the con-

---

and social benefits. This is one reason why the Bible can and does specify certain social policies. They are beneficial for the covenanted community. But Rothbard's logic is correct: in terms of the presuppositions of modern, subjectivist economics, there is no way to add up subjective costs or benefits. In fact, consistent reasoning leads us to conclude further that this conclusion applies to any attempt by economists scientifically to measure *intra*personal subjective utilities. Since actions and evaluations take place over time, economists would have to construct an "index number of personal satisfaction" – an impossibility, given the premises of subjective utility.

cept of social efficiency were meaningful, they don't answer the questions of why efficiency should be the overriding consideration in establishing legal principles or why externalities should be internalized above all other considerations.[4]

In an earlier essay, Rothbard presents perhaps the most comprehensive challenge to the whole economics profession that has ever been written. The reason why I quote him at length is that he is a very clear writer, and he is willing to follow the logic of subjectivist economics to great lengths – not to a biblical reconciliation of objective and subjective value, but at least to the far extremes of subjectivism. In a remarkable essay, "The Myth of Efficiency," Rothbard rejects not only social costs but the idea of efficiency:

> ... there are several layers of grave fallacy involved in the very concept of efficiency as applied to social institutions or policies: (1) the problem is not only in specifying ends but also in deciding *whose* ends are to be pursued; (2) individual ends are bound to conflict, and therefore any additive concept of social efficiency is meaningless; and (3) even each individual's actions cannot be assumed to be "efficient"; indeed, they undoubtedly will not be. Hence, efficiency is an erroneous concept even when applied to each individual's actions directed toward his ends; it is a fortiori a meaningless concept when it includes more than one individual, let alone an entire society.
>   Let us take a given individual. Since his own ends are clearly given and he acts to pursue them, surely at least *his* actions can be considered efficient? But no, they may not, for in order for him to act efficiently, he would have to possess perfect knowledge – perfect knowledge of the best technology, of future actions and reactions by other people, and of future natural events. But since no one can ever have perfect knowledge of the future,

---

4. Murray N. Rothbard, "Law, Property Rights, and Air Pollution," *Cato Journal*, II (Spring 1982), pp. 58-59.

no one's action can be called "efficient." We live in a world of uncertainty. Efficiency is therefore a chimera.

Put another way, action is a learning process. As the individual acts to achieve his ends, he learns and becomes more proficient about how to pursue them. But in that case, of course, his actions cannot have been efficient from the start – or even from the end – of his actions, since perfect knowledge is never achieved, and there is always more to learn.

Moreover, the individual's ends are not *really* given, for there is no reason to assume that they are set in concrete for all time. As the individual learns more about the world, about nature and about other people, his values and goals are bound to change. The individual's ends will change as he learns from other people; they may also change out of sheer caprice. But if ends change in the course of an action, the concept of efficiency – which can only be defined as the best combination of means in pursuit of given ends – again becomes meaningless.[5]

Two comments are in order. *First*, we can perceive the whole corpus of economics steadily slipping through our fingers. If the question of efficiency is meaningless, what have economists been arguing about over the last three centuries? An illusion? The answer must be *yes*, if we hold to a rigorously subjectivist epistemology. "Not only is 'efficiency' a myth, then, but so too is any concept of social or additive cost, or even an objectively determinable cost for each individual. But if cost is individual, ephemeral, and purely subjective, then it follows that no policy conclusions, including conclusions about law, can be derived from or even make use of such a concept. There can be no valid or meaningful cost-benefit analysis of political or legal decisions or institutions."[6] Rothbard has shown the intellectual courage to affirm the validity of the implications that Roy Har-

---

5. Murray N. Rothbard, "Comment: The Myth of Efficiency," in Mario J. Rizzo (ed.), *Time, Uncertainty, and Disequilibrium* (Lexington, Massachusetts: Lexington Books, 1979), p. 90.

6. *Ibid.*, p. 94.

rod used to frighten Lionel Robbins away from his own denial of the possibility of making interpersonal comparisons of subjective utility. He denies the possibility of policy-making based on economics.

The Problem of Exhaustive Knowledge

Second, we discover in Rothbard's arguments against the concept of efficiency an argument based on the impossibility of using a concept which is only meaningful in an imaginary changeless world. This is a variation of an antinomy (logical contradiction) of humanism which Cornelius Van Til pointed to in several contexts, namely, that for the anti-theist, it is necessary to know everything exhaustively in order to know anything specifically. The heart of the problem, Van Til says, is that *there is no way for the anti-theist to integrate his timeless model of reality to the ceaseless flux of historical change.*

In contrast to the humanists, Van Til argues, Christians have God's revelation of Himself and His creation to guide them in making sense of this world, and "it is only by stressing the comprehensiveness and the inexhaustible character of the idea of revelation that the process of learning can have meaning and history have genuine significance. If man is made the final reference point in predication, knowledge cannot get under way, and if it could get under way it could not move forward. That is to say, in all non-Christian forms of epistemology there is first the idea that to be understood a fact must be understood exhaustively. It must be reducible to a part of a system of timeless logic. But man himself and the facts of his experience are subject to change. How is he ever to find within himself an a priori resting point? He himself is on the move. . . . Every effort of man to find one spot that he can exhaustively understand either in the world of fact about him or in the world of experience within, is doomed to failure. If we do not with Calvin presuppose the self-contained God back of the self-conscious act of the knowing mind of man, we are doomed to be lost in an endless and bottomless flux."[7]

The economist faces this problem continually; it cannot be overcome logically. Because the Austrian School of economics focuses above all on two fundamental questions – subjective knowledge (e.g., valuations) and purposeful human action (e.g., the market process over time) – "Austrians" have devoted more space than most economists to discussions of the interrelations between historical change and economic knowledge. Members of the Austrian School understand that the model used to undergird all modern economic theory, namely, the general equilibrium model, hypothesizes a world of perfect foreknowledge, and therefore zero uncertainty, a world in which human action cannot even be conceived.[8] Mario J. Rizzo says that "general equilibrium exists in the mind of the economist and not in the real world."[9] Rothbard agrees: ". . . not only has it never existed, and is not an operational concept, but also it could not conceivably exist. For we cannot really conceive of a world where every person has perfect foresight, and where no data ever change. . . ."[10]

This raises a crucial problem for the economist: the problem of objective cost. Buchanan summarizes this problem: "One of the central confusions leading to the false objectification of costs has been the extension of the perfect knowledge assumption of competitive equilibrium theory to the analysis of nonequilibrium choices, whether made in a market or nonmarket process.

---

7. Cornelius Van Til, *An Introduction to Systematic Theology*, vol. V of *In Defense of Biblical Christianity* (Phillipsburg, New Jersey: Presbyterian & Reformed, 1978), pp. 166-67.

8. Mises, *Human Action* (3rd ed.; Chicago: Regnery, 1966), p. 248. For my comments on Mises, see Gary North, *The Dominion Covenant: Genesis* (2nd ed; Tyler, Texas: Institute for Christian Economics, 1987), p. 352.

9. Mario J. Rizzo, "Uncertainty, Subjectivity, and the Economic Analysis of the Law," in Rizzo (ed.), *Time, Uncertainty*, p. 82.

10. *Ibid.*, p. 93. Cf. Buchanan, *Cost and Choice: An Inquiry in Economic Theory* (Chicago: University of Chicago Press, 1969), p. 98.

Genuine choice is confronted only in a world of uncertainty, and, of course, all economic choices are made in this context."[11] Take away equilibrium – from men's thinking, that is; it never has existed in the real world – and you thereby eliminate the economist's concept of objective cost. Eliminate the concept of objective cost, and you eliminate the possibility of scientifically valid policy-making by economists. Eliminate the concept of objective cost, and you also eliminate that trusty ideological weapon of all free market economists: the idea of the objective efficiency of the free market.

Efficiency for Whose Ends?

Here is the problem Rothbard is struggling with: How can we discuss the question of efficiency – the coherence of planning and action – in a context of *change*, both with respect to a man's plans and the environment which he attempts to change and yet also must respond to. Rothbard wants to believe that he can appeal to what he calls "proficiency" in learning, but his critique of efficiency applies equally well to proficiency. Why is human action a learning process? Why does anything we learned a decade, a year, or a moment ago still apply in the now-changed world of the present? Humanists have no answer to this fundamental question, at least none which is consistent with their epistemology of autonomous man.

Rothbard argues correctly that "efficiency only makes sense in regard to people's ends, and individuals' ends differ, clash, and conflict. The central question of politics then becomes: *whose* ends shall rule?"[12] He attacks modern economics because it is based on *utilitarianism* – "the greatest good for the greatest number" – a system of ethics which assumes that it is possible to make interpersonal comparisons of subjective utility. Utilitarianism ultimately asserts that there is a *universal common*

---

11. Buchanan, *Cost and Choice*, p. 98; cf. pp. 49-50.
12. Rothbard, "Comment," *Time, Uncertainty*, p. 91.

ethical system and a *universal hierarchy of values*, for if there were not, it would be impossible for social planners to devise and enforce social policies. "For utilitarianism holds that everyone's ends are *really* the same, and that therefore all social conflict is merely technical and pragmatic, and can be resolved once the appropriate means for the common ends are discovered and adopted. It is the myth of the common universal end that allows economists to believe that they can 'scientifically' and in a supposedly value-free manner prescribe what political policies should be adopted. By taking this alleged common universal end as an unquestioned given, the economist allows himself the delusion that he is not at all a moralist but only a strictly value-free and professional technician."[13]

Rothbard gives an example of the problem of social efficiency. What if one group in society wishes to exterminate all members of a rival group? "In these cases of conflicting ends, furthermore, one group's 'efficiency' becomes another group's detriment. So that the advocates of a program – whether of compulsory uniformity or of slaughtering a defined social group – would want their proposals carried out as efficiently as possible; whereas, on the other hand, the oppressed group would hope for as *in*efficient a pursuit of the hated goal as possible. Efficiency, as Rizzo points out, can only be meaningful relative to a given goal of the acting individual. But if ends clash, the opposing group will favor maximum *in*efficiency in pursuit of the disliked goal. Efficiency, therefore, can never serve as a utilitarian touchstone for law or public policy."[14]

Rothbard's conclusion is extremely important for a study of Christian economics. By systematically destroying the epistemological foundation for efficiency as a concept of subjectivist economics, he is then faced with a major question: What is the proper foundation for social policy? As an anarchist, he does

---

13. *Idem.*
14. *Ibid.*, pp. 91-92.

not believe in social policy, meaning a State-enforced policy. He wants the market's forces to arbitrate in deciding whose plans become dominant at any point in time. But even these plans cannot be based on questions of efficiency, as he well knows. He then calls for a restructuring of economic thought – a reformation based on *ethics*.

> I conclude that we cannot decide on public policy, tort law, rights, or liabilities on the basis of efficiencies or minimizing of costs. But if not costs or efficiency, then what? The answer is that only *ethical principles* can serve as criteria for our decisions. Efficiency can never serve as the basis for ethics; on the contrary, ethics must be the guide and touchstone for any consideration of efficiency. Ethics is the primary. . . .
>
> One group of people will inevitably balk at our conclusion; I speak, of course, of the economists. For in this area economists have been long engaged in what George Stigler, in another context, has called "intellectual imperialism."[15] Economists will have to get used to the idea that not all of life can be encompassed by our own discipline. A painful lesson no doubt, but compensated by the knowledge that it may be good for our souls to realize our own limits – and, just perhaps, to learn about ethics and about justice.[16]

This represents a major break from contemporary economics, even from Austrian School economics. Rothbard is no lon-

---

15. Rothbard attributes the phrase to George Stigler, but Kenneth Boulding is better known for its use, by which he means "an attempt on the part of economics to take over all the other social sciences." Boulding, "Economics As A Moral Science," *American Economic Review*, LIX (March 1969), p. 8.

16. *Ibid.*, p. 95. Rothbard is an advocate of a universal ethics based on natural rights. See *For a New Liberty: The Libertarian Manifesto* (rev. ed.; New York: Collier, 1978), pp. 15, 26-28, 134, 239. Not all "Austrians" share his confidence in natural rights and natural law as the basis of a universal ethics, as John Eggar points out: "Comment: Efficiency Is Not a Substitute for Ethics," in Rizzo (ed.), *Time, Uncertainty*, p. 119. For critiques of natural law doctrines from a biblical viewpoint, see the essays by John Robbins, Rex Downie, and Archie Jones in *Journal of Christian Reconstruction*, V (Summer 1978): "Symposium on Politics."

ger willing to affirm, as Mises the utilitarian affirmed, that "when the superior efficiency of economic freedom could no longer be questioned, social philosophy entered the scene and demolished the ideology of the status system."[17] The debate over the free market is over ethics, not economic efficiency.[18]

Methodology: Ethics vs. Efficiency

Rothbard's straightforward abandonment of the concept of efficiency, and his call to economists to examine ethics as the source of their policy judgments, are significant intellectual developments. They constitute an admission that there is something dangerously wrong with the economists' reliance on the rational model of equilibrium. If a methodology based on the idea of economic equilibrium cannot be relied upon to solve questions of economic efficiency, then in what way can it safely be used by economists? Rothbard is calling into question the most important intellectual and technical tool that the economist has at his disposal, the "ideal type" of the perfectly competitive economy.[19] Challenge this, and you challenge the epistemological foundation of modern economic science.

---

17. Mises, *The Ultimate Foundation of Economic Science* (Princeton, New Jersey: Van Nostrand, 1962), p. 109.

18. F. A. Harper told me that he had pressed Mises to answer this question: "If the socialist economy were more efficient than the free market, would you favor socialism?" Mises replied: "But it isn't more efficient." Harper repeated the question, and Mises repeated the answer. Harper said that Mises' utilitarian defense of the free market made him blind to the ethical issue between socialism and the free market economy, which Harper regarded as the fundamental issue.

19. Perhaps the most influential explanation of the use of "ideal types" or hypothetical abstract models in the social sciences was offered by Max Weber. See Weber's book, *The Methodology of the Social Sciences*, translated and edited by Edward A. Shils and Henry A. Finch (New York: Free Press, 1949), pp. 43-45, 87-105. See also Thomas Burger, *Max Weber's Theory of Concept Formation: History, Laws and Ideal Types* (Durham, North Carolina: Duke University Press, 1976); Rolf E. Rogers, *Max Weber's Ideal Type Theory* (New York: Philosophical Library, 1969); Julien Freund, *The Sociology of Max Weber* (New York: Pantheon, 1968), pp. 59-70; Raymond Aron, "The Logic of the Social Sciences," in Denis Wrong (ed.), *Max Weber* (Englewood Cliffs, New Jersey: Prentice-Hall, 1970), pp. 80-89.

Yet it must be challenged. More than this: *it must be scrapped*. The search for a timeless, rational mental construct as the basis of a science of human action is fruitless. Even the great Mises was partially sidetracked by this quest. What confidence can we legitimately have in an explanation of market processes which argues that as entrepreneurship becomes successful, it "tends toward" the creation of a world in which human action and human choice is impossible, a world of automatons rather than people? Yet this is the explanatory model used by Mises (and almost all other economists). As he says in *Human Action* concerning his theoretical construct, the Evenly Rotating Economy: "Action is change, and change is the temporal sequence. But in the evenly rotating economy change and succession of events are eliminated. Action is to make choices and to cope with an uncertain future. But in the evenly rotating economy there is no choosing and the future is not uncertain as it does not differ from the present known state. Such a rigid system is not peopled with living men making choices and liable to error; it is a world of soulless unthinking automatons; it is not a human society, it is an ant hill."[20] Nevertheless, he states flatly: "The theorems implied in the notion of the plain state of rest are valid with regard to all transactions without exception."[21] For the modern economist, all human action tends toward a final state in which human beings become omniscient and therefore take on one of the attributes of God.[22] The problem is, their view of God is that He could not possibly act if He existed. He would be a "rule-following automaton,"[23] because "A perfect being would not act."[24]

---

20. Mises, *Human Action*, p. 248.
21. *Ibid.*, p. 245.
22. Mises writes: "No matter whether this thirsting after omniscience can ever be fully gratified or not, man will not cease to strive after it passionately." Mises, *Ultimate Foundation*, p. 120.
23. Buchanan, *Cost and Choice*, p. 96.
24. Mises, *Epistemological Problems of Economics* (Princeton, New Jersey: Van

Timeless Metaphysical Models

Mises relies on this limiting concept of a hypothetical economy filled with soulless people in order to explain the operations of real-world market forces. "This final state of rest is an imaginary construction, not a description of reality. For the final state of rest will never be attained. New disturbing factors will emerge before it will be realized. What makes it necessary to take recourse to this imaginary construction is the fact that the market at every instant is moving toward a final state of rest."[25] He calls this movement toward (or "tendency toward") a final state of rest a *fact*. But this "fact" is precisely what must be demonstrated.[26] It is the economists' version of the familiar pre-Socratic contradiction between Parmenides' changeless and timeless logic and Heraclitus' ceaseless historical flow. These two worlds cannot be shown to be connected; nevertheless, they are correlative in the thinking of humanistic scholars.

To explain this intellectual dilemma, Van Til uses the delightful analogy of someone who is trying to put together a string of beads, but the string is infinitely long, and the beads have no holes. The imaginary world of timeless logic (Van Til's "string") which cannot possibly exist serves as the *limiting concept* (to use Kant's terminology for the "noumenal"),[27] or *limiting notion* (to use Mises' term)[28] for our understanding of the world which does exist – the world of ceaseless flux (Van Til's "beads"). This world of timeless logic is, in short, a logical backdrop which cannot ever exist in the real world – and which

---

Nostrand, 1960), p. 24. Cf. Mises, *Ultimate Foundation*, p. 3.

25. *Idem.*

26. The problem Mises is dealing with is the problem of analyzing change in terms of fixed mental categories. "There is no means of studying the complex phenomena of action other than first to abstract from change altogether, then to introduce an isolated factor provoking change, and ultimately to analyze its effects under the assumption that other things remain equal." Mises, *Human Action*, p. 248.

27. Immanuel Kant, *Critique of Pure Reason*, translated by Norman Kemp Smith (New York: St. Martin's, [1929] 1965), B311, p. 272.

28. Mises, *Human Action*, p. 249.

really cannot even be mentally conceived[29] – which is used to explain the world inhabited by men.

Nevertheless, with absolute confidence (even "apodictic certainty," one of Mises' favorite terms), Mises proclaims that "These insoluble contradictions, however, do not affect the service which this imaginary construction renders...."[30] Or even more forcefully: "Even imaginary constructions which are inconceivable, self-contradictory, or unrealizable can render useful, even indispensable services in the comprehension of reality, provided the economist knows how to use them properly."[31] That word, "provided," covers a multitude of epistemological sins. So does the word "properly."

Anyone who has ever tried to read an article in such journals as *Econometrica* and *The Review of Economics and Statistics* knows how rarified economic logic can become.[32] It reminds me of what little I know about the formal academic debates carried on by the late medieval scholastics. The number of angels dancing on the point of a needle is a down-to-earth problem compared to stochastic analysis applied to a world of perfect foreknowledge. The *sophistication* of modern econometric analysis is

---

29. How can we imagine a world in which every actor has perfect foreknowledge? Try to explain the meaning of human choice in a world in which everyone knows in advance precisely what the others will inevitably do in the future. We may take such a world on faith; we cannot explain it.

30. *Ibid.*, p. 248. He writes: "The method of imaginary constructions is indispensable for praxeology [the science of human action -- G.N.]; it is the only method of praxeological and economic inquiry. It is, to be sure, a method difficult to handle because it can easily result in fallacious syllogisms. It leads along a sharp edge; on both sides yawns the chasm of absurdity and nonsense. Only merciless self-criticism can prevent a man from falling headlong into these abysmal depths." *Ibid.*, p. 237. Question: Self-criticism in terms of what truth, or by what standard? For a critique of this position, see North, *Dominion Covenant: Genesis*, pp. 352-53.

31. Mises, *ibid.*, p. 236.

32. I do not have in mind merely the writings of Nobel Prize-winning economist Gerard Debreu, which do not pretend to deal with the real world. I have in mind investigations into the operation of real-world institutions, such as William M. Landes, "An Economic Analysis of the Courts," *Journal of Law & Economics*, XIV (April 1971), pp. 61-107.

matched ("correlation of at least .9") only by the *irrelevance* of its conclusions.

Conclusion

The dilemma faced by modern economists is to explain the time-bound, uncertainty-bound processes of the market in terms of timeless logical categories ("models"). They try to explain change in terms of fixed laws, time in terms of timelessness, uncertainty in terms of omniscience (i.e., equilibrium conditions). They need to show how the concept of efficiency applies to (1) objective, real-world decisions of men and (2) subjectivist economic theory. They need to show how policy-making can be abstracted from both ethics and the concept of objective value. They need to show how social cost is a legitimate extension of the idea of subjective cost. They need to show how expected costs can be linked to retrospective costs, both individual and social.

Economists have long assumed not only that these epistemological problems can somehow be solved some day in terms of modern economic theory, but more to the point, that these problems can safely be ignored until that later day. Economists have quietly dropped any public discussion of these problems until that day arrives. But that later day is the equivalent of the advent of equilibrium: a theoretical limiting concept, not a target date. Meanwhile, the blessed ones deposit their objective Nobel Prize checks in the local objective bank accounts. Nice work if you can get it.

Rothbard has faced this crucial epistemological limit on the science of economics: "I contend that no advocacy of public policy, however seemingly 'scientific,' can be value free; none can escape taking an ethical position. Far better, then, to frame one's ethics clearly and consciously, instead of smuggling them in, ad hoc and unanalyzed, as implicit assumptions of one's analysis."[33] Economic analysis informs us that the reason why smuggling exists is because of controls that inhibit voluntary exchange. In this case, the control is the economics profession's ban on open discussions of this question: *ethics as an inescapable aspect of policy-making*. Rothbard has called attention to the epistemologically soft underbelly of the economics profession: the myth of ethical neutrality in economics. This is another reason why he is not going to win the Nobel Prize.[34]

---

33. Rothbard, "Introduction to the French Edition of *Ethics of Liberty*," *Journal of Libertarian Studies*, X (Fall 1991), p. 14.

34. Gary North, "Why Murray Rothbard Will Never Win the Nobel Prize!" *Man, Economy, and Liberty: Essays in Honor of Murray N. Rothbard*, edited by Walter Block and Llewellyn H. Rockwell, Jr. (Auburn, Alabama: Ludwig von Mises Institute, 1988), ch. 8.

5

"WEIGHING UP THE GAINS AND LOSSES"

> *Almost always the men who achieve these fundamental inventions of a new paradigm have been either very young or very new to the field whose paradigm they change. And perhaps that point need not have been made explicit, for obviously these are the men who, being little committed by prior practice to the traditional rules of normal science, are particularly likely to see that those rules no longer define a playable game and to conceive another set that can replace them.*
>
> Thomas Kuhn[1]

Coase's theorem deliberately ignores the ethical question of private property rights and the losses to those whose rights are violated. "It is all a question of weighing up the gains that would accrue from eliminating these harmful effects against the gains that accrue from allowing them to continue."[2] But here is the *real* "problem of social costs": *the economist, as a scientist, has no way to "weigh up" economic gains and losses.*[3] Here is the root of the epistemological crisis of modern economics.

---

1. Thomas Kuhn, *The Structure of Scientific Revolutions* (Chicago: University of Chicago Press, 1962), p. 91.
2. Coase, "Social Cost," p. 26.
3. Gary North, *The Dominion Covenant: Genesis* (2nd ed; Tyler, Texas: Institute for Christian Economics, 1987), ch. 4.

Coase and all of his followers go on blithely as if all this talk about tallying up costs and benefits – social or individual – has any epistemologically valid theoretical meaning for a methodological individualist, let alone any scientific application. He writes: "The problem which we face in dealing with actions which have harmful effects is not simply one of restraining those responsible for them. What has to be decided is whether the gain from preventing the harm is greater than the loss which would be suffered elsewhere as a result of stopping the action which produces the harm."[4] *But economists cannot measure social costs and benefits, according to the logic of modern economics, since costs and benefits are exclusively subjective categories.*

Humanistic economists go about their business as if "equilibrium analysis" were anything more than a teaching device, and very often a misleading one.[5] The assumptions of equilibrium analysis deny the possibility of human action in a world in which these equilibrium conditions exist. Why? Because there is perfect knowledge for market participants in such a universe, and therefore neither profits nor losses. (Yet even under equilibrium, there would be transaction costs. There are no free lunches in the land of equilibrium; it is just that everyone knows exactly how much lunch will cost.) This is a world of automatons, not humans, as Mises wrote. Yet all of the "rigorously scientific" discussions of economic efficiency and optimal distribution are based on the trans-historical model of equilibrium.

Peter Lewin has seen this fact more clearly than most economists have: "The other important assumption underlying the efficiency approach is the absence of significant distortions elsewhere in the economy. The calculation of social costs and

---

4. Coase, "Social Cost," p. 27.

5. Debreau's mathematical analysis of free market equilibrium may have won him the 1983 Nobel Prize in economics, but it tells us little about how the real world of supply and demand actually works. Gerard Debreau, *Theory of Price: An Axiomatic Analysis of Equilibrium* (New Haven, Connecticut: Yale University Press, 1959). What is needed are defenses based on real-world categories.

benefits is profoundly affected if this assumption is violated. In a world of distortions, where prices are not general equilibrium competitive prices that reflect marginal costs, the imposition of a Pigouvian tax or a liability that would achieve efficiency if distortions were absent may *reduce* efficiency. . . . In more general terms, outside of equilibrium there is no way to know if any move is efficiency-enhancing or not."[6] He goes so far as to say – quite accurately with respect to a methodology devoid of the concept of God, revelation, and absolute objective values – that "the notion of efficiency makes little sense outside of general equilibrium."[7]

Coase is unquestionably correct that "In a world in which there are costs of rearranging the rights established by the legal system, the courts, in cases relating to nuisance, are, in effect, making a decision on the economic problem and determining how resources are to be employed."[8] To the extent that Coase's article helps judges or others to become more aware of this inescapable reality of economic allocation, it is a useful essay. But how useful is a rarified academic exercise which overlooks that most fundamental of economic costs: *the cost of suffering a violation of justice?* Never forget: he wants to limit his discussion to costs and benefits, "questions of equity apart."

Optimal Crime and Optimal Punishment

We see the same sort of "add it up" reasoning in a subdivision of law and economics: crime and punishment. Ever since Gary S. Becker's pioneering article in 1968, University of Chicago-type economists have been analyzing crime and law enforcement in terms of a model that minimizes social losses from crime. This model treats social costs and optimal social solutions

---

6. Peter Lewin, "Pollution Externalities: Social Cost and Strict Liability," *Cato Journal*, II (Spring 1982), pp. 216-17.
7. *Ibid.*, p. 217.
8. Coase, "Social Cost," p. 27.

as if such concepts had scientific validity in a world of subjectivist economic analysis. Please forgive the following; it was written by an economist:

> Optimal policies are defined as those that minimize the social loss from crime. That loss depends upon the net damage to victims; the resource costs of discovering, apprehending, and convicting offenders; and the costs of punishment itself. These components of the loss, in turn, depend upon the number of criminal offenders, the probability of apprehending and convicting offenders, the size and form of punishments, the potential legal incomes of offenders, and several other variables. The optimal supply of criminal offenses – in essence, the amount of crime – is then determined by selecting values for the probability of conviction, the penalty, and other variables determined by society that minimize the social loss from crime. Within this framework, theorems are derived that relate the optimal probability of conviction, the optimal punishments, and the optimal supply of criminal offenses to such factors as the size of the damages from various types of crimes, changes in the overall costs of apprehending and convicting offenders, and differences in the relative responsiveness of offenders to conviction probabilities and to penalties.[9]

This all sounds so scientific, but it is all spurious if economics does not allow the interpersonal comparison of subjective utilities or the aggregating of interpersonal utilities, which it does not. But sophisticated, intellectually rigorous analyses such as this certainly do increase the likelihood of academic tenure and personal career advancement for those who get such things published – an employment guarantee that some people (myself included) regard as less than socially optimal.[10]

---

9. William M. Landes, in Gary S. Becker and William M. Landes (eds.), *Essays in the Economics of Crime and Punishment* (New York: National Bureau of Economic Research, 1974), p. xiv. Each of the five authors who contributed the book's six essays was at the time a professor at the University of Chicago.

10. Cf. Robert A. Nisbet, "The Permanent Professors: A Modest Proposal," *Public*

What the reader should be aware of is that the practitioners of economics are unhappy with the public's perception of their trade. On the one hand, the economist as rigorous scientist cannot do without the concept of equilibrium to build his theories, and this concept begins with the presupposition of perfect, zero-cost knowledge. Then the economist attempts to impose this equilibrium model onto the error-filled real world, "making appropriate modifications," of course. Problem: the moment you make any modification, the model disintegrates. At best, the equilibrium model is useful as a platform for making intuitive leaps of faith. Intuitive leaps of faith are inescapable aspects of all economic thought, but they are something that economists prefer not to discuss, even in private.[11]

Becker's Breakthrough

Gary Becker insists that his approach to crime and punishment does not "assume perfect knowledge, lightning-fast calculation, or any of the other caricatures of economic theory."[12] Dr. Becker is self-deceived; this is exactly what all discussions of socially optimum decision-making must assume. This so-called caricature is in fact the heart, mind, and soul of modern economics as an academic discipline. Without it, there could be no mathematics or equations in economic analysis, and without mathematics, one rarely gets into print in the prestigious scholarly economics journals.[13] Certainly, Dr. Becker's essay is made nearly unreadable by page after page of pseudo-scientific equations, as are most of his other essays. (I have decided to

---

Interest (Fall 1965); reprinted in Nisbet, *Tradition and Revolt: Historical and Sociological Essays* (New York: Random House, 1968), ch. 12.

11. North, "Economics: From Reason to Intuition," in North (ed.), *Foundations of Christian Scholarship* (Vallecito, California: Ross House, 1976), ch. 5.

12. Gary S. Becker, "Crime and Punishment: an Economic Approach" (1968), in *Essays in the Economics of Crime and Punishment*, p. 9.

13. John Kenneth Galbraith, *Economics Peace and Laughter* (Boston: Houghton Mifflin, 1971), ch. 2.

coin a new adjective that describes this pseudo-scientific approach to economic reasoning: *psientific*.)

Becker insists that "This essay concentrates almost entirely on determining optimal policies to combat illegal behavior and pays little attention to actual policies."[14] In this regard, the essay is representative of virtually the whole field of law and economics. Becker prefers equations and equilibrium to personal responsibility when it comes to suggesting what should be done about crime. He and his colleagues refuse to honor Baird's warning: "Since all costs and benefits are subjective, no government can accurately identify, much less establish, the optimum quantity of anything."[15] Admit this, and 90 percent of what gets published in the professional academic journals would have to be rejected by the editors. Where, under such academically sub-optimal circumstances, would a career economist publish an essay such as Isaac Ehrlich's representative example, "Optimal Participation in Illegitimate Market Activities: A One-Period Uncertainty Model"?[16]

Biblical law is the foundation of optimal social and economic policies – the *only* foundation that honors God and can therefore produce long-term benefits: covenantal blessings. This is why we need to adhere to the Bible's system of penalties to be imposed by the civil government; without this, we are flying blind. We are flying as blind as Gary Becker is when he writes: "A wise use of fines requires knowledge of marginal gains and harm and of marginal apprehension and conviction costs; admittedly, such knowledge is not easily attained."[17] *Not easily attained!* In terms of the logic of subjective economics, such

---

14. *Essays in the Economics of Crime and Punishment*, p. 44.

15. Charles W. Baird, "The Philosophy and Ideology of Pollution Regulation," *Cato Journal*, II (Spring 1982), p. 303.

16. Actually, this was only a subsection in his influential and equation-filled article, "Participation in Illegitimate Activities: An Economic Analysis," in *Essays in the Economics of Crime and Punishment*.

17. Becker, in *ibid.*, p. 28.

knowledge cannot be attained at all. We cannot make scientific interpersonal comparisons of subjective utility or disutility. Professional economists may shudder at the thought of restructuring civil sanctions to make civil law conform more closely to God's revealed law, but they have nothing to offer in its place except endless self-deception regarding the scientific possibility of discovering socially optimal levels of crime and punishment.[18]

Becker's essay does not even consider the possibility of restitution payments by criminals to their victims, but instead focuses on the social benefits of fines paid to the State. This is a remarkable lack of perception on his part, given his position as a representative of a free market school of thought that presumably opposes the expansion of the State. What mainly disturbs Becker is that with imprisonment, "some of the payment 'by' offenders would not be received by the rest of society, and a net social loss would result."[19] He is so concerned with questions of "net social loss" that he neglects the crucial question of the net *personal* loss suffered by the victim.[20] The word "restitution" does not appear in the index of *Essays in the Economics of Crime and Punishment*. (The book has approximately 170 pages of equations or parts of equations in its 273 pages, with most of the remainder devoted to charts, graphs, statistical regression analysis, brief bibliographies, and the five and a half page index

---

18. For example, Nobel Prize-winning University of Chicago economist George Stigler's essay, "The Optimum Enforcement of Laws," *ibid*, pp. 55-67.

19. *Ibid.*, pp. 24-25.

20. He says that criminal law should deal only with crimes in which victims cannot be compensated. "Thus an action would be 'criminal' precisely because it results in uncompensated 'harm' to others." *Ibid.*, p. 33. I have some questions. First, if someone can serve a prison term or pay a fine to the State, why can't he compensate victims instead? Second, why does Becker refuse to discuss the overwhelming majority of crimes in which there are identifiable victims, preferring instead to fill up pages with equations? Is he conveniently defining away the problem of crime and punishment for the vast majority of crimes? Third, why does he feel it necessary to put quotation marks around *criminal* and *harm*? Is it because such language smacks too much of objective moral norms?

in which the word "restitution" does not appear.)[21] Two decades later, Becker is still humming the same old tune: "deterrence, not vengeance," fines, not restitution to victims. And he still has discovered no objective answer to the problem he raises: making the punishment fit the crime: "Obviously, it is hard to estimate damages for many company crimes and even harder to determine the probability of conviction."[22] Hard? By the standards of subjective value theory, *it is theoretically impossible*. Yet Chicago School economists refuse to admit this in print.

Buchanan is correct in his discussion of the economics of crime: ". . . any costs which the economist may objectify need bear little relation to those costs which serve as actual obstacles to decisions." He is not correct, however, in his next sentence: "Recognition of this fact need not destroy the usefulness of the economic analysis."[23] Without a scientifically verifiable link between subjective decision-making and objective fines, the economist cannot make a coherent case for any outcome other than judicial chaos. (It should not be surprising that Becker has argued that the free market would bring economic order even if all men's decisions were irrational.)[24] The economist needs a ruler, as Thirlby has so accurately identified it. In fact, he capitalizes it.[25] The economist does indeed need a Ruler, an "omniscient observer who can read all preference functions," as Buchanan so professionally describes Him.[26] But economists

---

21. For an equally arcane academic treatment, see David J. Pyle, *The Economics of Crime and Law Enforcement* (New York: St. Martin's, 1983).

22. Gary Becker, "Make the Punishment Fit the Corporate Crime," *Business Week* (March 13, 1989).

23. James Buchanan, *Cost and Choice: An Inquiry in Economic Theory* (Chicago: University of Chicago Press, 1969), p. 93.

24. Gary Becker, "Irrational Behavior and Economic Theory," *Journal of Political Economy*, LXX (Feb. 1962). For my critique of his position, as well as Israel Kirzner's very different critique, see North, *Dominion Covenant*, pp. 347-53.

25. Thirlby, "The Ruler," *South African Journal of Economics*, XIV (Dec. 1946), reprinted in *L.S.E. Essays on Cost* (New York: New York University Press, 1981).

26. Buchanan, *Cost and Choice*, p. 95.

have denied His relevance from the beginning of the profession; economics was the first scientific guild to do so. It was this self-conscious separation of economics from both theology and morality that economist William Letwin praises as "the greatest accomplishment of the seventeenth century."[27] (It apparently overshadowed the less significant work of Director of the Mint Mr. Newton.)

This digression has been necessary in order to demonstrate what the academic field of economics and law is really all about. It is all about making scholarly reputations and making preposterous assumptions. The more preposterous the assumptions, the more scholarly the reputation. And it is all done in the name of optimality: "The main contribution of this essay, as I see it, is to demonstrate that optimal policies to combat illegal behavior are part of an optimal allocation of resources."[28]

The Social Benefits of Criminal Behavior

A unique component of the Becker thesis on criminal behavior is his thesis that the concern of society in prohibiting criminal behavior ought to be the reduction of *net* social cost. This is a very important qualification. In calculating the net cost to society of any criminal act, *Becker insists that we must count as a positive benefit the gains made by the criminal by committing the crime.* "The net cost or damage to society is simply the difference between the harm and gain," he writes.[29] How can he say this? Because of his thesis – the one which undergirds this whole subdivision of economics – that *criminal behavior is no different from any other profit-seeking behavior*. Ethics has no role to play in distinguishing crime from other profit-seeking activities. "The approach taken here follows the economists' usual analysis of

---

27. William Letwin, *The Origins of Scientific Economics* (Garden City, New York: Doubleday Anchor, [1963] 1965), p. 159.
28. Becker, "Crime and Punishment," *op. cit.*, p. 45.
29. *Ibid.*, p. 6.

choice and assumes that a person commits an offense if the expected utility to him exceeds the utility he could get by using his time and other resources at other activities. Some persons become 'criminals,' therefore, not because their basic motivation differs from that of other persons, but because their benefits and costs differ."[30]

Notice, first, that he puts the word *criminals* in quotation marks, indicating his fear of making an ethical judgment in a scholarly journal. Second, he hesitates to follow what economists sometimes call the pure logic of choice.[31] He says that *some* persons become criminals "because their benefits and costs differ" from law-abiding persons. Why not use cost-benefit analysis to explain the actions of *all* criminals? Why limit it to only *some*? Why bother to distinguish the non-economic motives of criminals from those of non-criminals? The logic of his argument is that non-economic motives and personal tastes are irrelevant for economic analysis; only costs and benefits are relevant for making predictions regarding people's economic behavior.[32] Why not follow the logic of the argument? Why

---

30. *Ibid.*, p. 9.

31. F. A. Hayek, "Economics and Knowledge," *Economica*, IV (1937), reprinted in Hayek, *Individualism and Economic Order* (Chicago: University of Chicago Press, 1948), pp. 35, 39, 46-47. See also Richard Fuerle, *The Pure Logic of Choice* (New York: Vantage, 1986).

32. This is how professional economists assess Becker's argument. Writes Paul H. Rubin: "Becker essentially argued that criminals are about like anyone else – that is, they rationally maximize their own self-interest (utility) subject to the constraints (prices, incomes) that they face in the marketplace and elsewhere. Thus the decision to become a criminal is in principle no different from the decision to become a bricklayer or a carpenter, or, indeed, an economist. The individual considers the net costs and benefits of each alternative and makes his decision on this basis. If we then want to explain changes in criminal behavior over time or space, we examine changes in these constraints. The basic assumption in this type of research is that tastes are constant and that changes in behavior can be explained by changes in prices." But we all know that tastes do change. This is economically irrelevant, say the economists. Why? Because economics cannot yet deal with changes in taste. "Tastes are assumed to be constant because we have absolutely no theory of changes in tastes. . . ." Rubin, "The Economics of Crime," in Ralph Andreano and John J. Siegfried (eds.), *The Economics of Crime* (New York: Wiley, 1980), p. 15.

not conclude in print that there is no theoretically valid economic difference between profit-seeking activities and criminal acts; there are only differences in net social utility? But he does not go this far. It is almost as if some last remaining trace of common sense and moral values has kept Dr. Becker from pursuing the logic of his position.

His followers have not been so reticent: "An individual decision to commit a crime (or not to commit a crime) is simply an application of the economist's theory of choice. If the benefits of the illegal action exceed the costs, the crime is committed, and it is not if costs exceed benefits. Offenders are not pictured as 'sick' or 'irrational,' but merely as engaging in activities that yield the most satisfaction, given their available alternatives."[33] Then what of the warning of God in Proverbs? "All they that hate me love death" (8:36b). Of course: just redefine suicidal criminal behavior in terms of the criminal's subjective preference for death, assume the existence of subjective ordinal (or even cardinal) utility in his subjective value preference scale, and economic analysis still holds! Common sense disappears, but economic analysis, like the smile of the cheshire cat, remains. (In all honesty, this kind of economic analysis goes back to the late eighteenth century. Jeremy Bentham used a very similar approach based on net pleasure or pain. Mercifully, the academic world had not yet discovered either econometrics or multivariate regression analysis, so his essays were literate and coherent.)

Becker was too timid to pursue his remarkable thesis very far. Let me show you where it leads. What about the net social cost or net social benefit of murder? He writes that "the cost of murder is measured by the loss of earnings of victims and excludes, among other things, the value placed by society on

---

33. Morgan O. Reynolds, "The Economics of Criminal Activity" (1973), reprinted in *ibid.*, p. 34.

life itself. . . ."³⁴ But this is insufficiently rigorous by the standards of Chicago School economics. He forgot that the victim's ability to earn a living also involves costs. The producer must eat, use public facilities of various kinds, and be a life-long absorber of resources. So, what Becker really meant to say is that the cost of murder is the net loss – discounted by the prevailing rate of long-term interest, of course[35] – of the late victim's lifetime earning potential, *minus* net lifetime expenditures (also discounted). This raises a key question in our era of legalized abortion, which may be a preliminary to legalized euthanasia (as it has been in the Netherlands): *What if the dead victim had been sick, dying, mentally retarded, or in some other way is a net absorber of society's scarce economic resources?* Must we not conclude that the murderer has in fact increased the net wealth of society? Remember Becker's rule: "society's" estimation of net social costs or benefits "excludes, among other things, the value placed by society on life itself." On what economic grounds could a legislator oppose the concept of selective murder, with criminal indictments to be handed down in specific cases only after a retrospective evaluation (by some committee or other) of net costs and benefits?[36] Who is to say? After all, as he says,

---

34. Becker, "Crime and Punishment," p. 9.

35. Richard A. Posner, *Economic Analysis of Law* (Boston: Little, Brown, 1986), pp. 170-81.

36. Becker also fails to mention the value of life to the late victim, which seems a bit odd, given the fact that Becker also pioneered a subdivision in the economics profession called human capital: Gary S. Becker, *Human Capital* (New York: National Bureau of Economic Research, 1964). Fortunately, Richard Posner has attempted to rectify this gaping hole in Becker's analysis. He does try to make an objective estimation of the economic value of life to the victim, which he concludes is nearly infinite. He uses a hypothetical example of rising economic payment that someone would demand to induce him to get involved in death-producing activities: the more likely death becomes, the higher the pay demanded. If death is sure, the price demanded will approach infinity. (Why, then, do men volunteer for suicide missions in wartime?) This is his surrogate for making a subjective posthumous estimation of life's monetary value to the late victim: Posner, *Economic Analysis of Law*, pp. 182-86. He draws no important conclusions from this analysis, however, and does not include it in his book's index under "death" or "death," for which there are no entries, or

"Reasonable men will often differ on the amount of damages or benefits caused by different activities."[37]

If all this begins to sound like the work of a madman, this is only because it is the work of a technically skilled University of Chicago economist who follows the logic of his position.[38] Bear in mind that Becker's essay on crime is regarded by his peers as a classic in the field, one comparable to (and written with the same presuppositions as) Coase's essay on social cost. One European economist has called Becker's work truly revolutionary. Even more: ". . . Gary Becker is classed among the greatest living American economists."[39]

Pin-Stickers and Their Victims

Becker has returned us to the age-old question of the pin-sticker and his victim.[40] If a person enjoys sticking pins into other people, and if other people resent this, what should society do? Construct a measuring device to record the joy of the pin-sticker and then compare it to the pain of his victim? Should society base the decision of whether to identify this act as a crime in terms of the pin-sticker's pleasure minus his victim's pain – "net social utility"? And if so, what do we do about the masochist who enjoys being stuck? (Yes, I know: sticking

---

under the entries for "murder."

37. Becker, "Crime and Punishment," p. 45.

38. For a brief, intelligent, and methodologically rigorous response to Becker, see G. Warren Nutter, "On Economism," *Journal of Law & Economics*, XXII (Oct. 1979), pp. 263-68. It was in response to Becker's methodology that I wrote my tongue-in-cheek piece, "A Note on the Opportunity Cost of Marriage," *Journal of Political Economy* (April 1968), in which I concluded that male Ph.D-holding scholars cannot afford to marry women who are not high school drop-outs. Astoundingly, George Stigler (seemingly straight-faced) replied in a subsequent issue that I had not dealt with Adam Smith accurately.

39. Henri Lepage, *Tomorrow, Capitalism: The Economics of Economic Freedom* (La Salle, Illinois: Open Court, [1978] 1982), p. 161. The chapter is titled, "The Gary Becker Revolution."

40. North, *Dominion Covenant*, pp. 44-45.

him would be a victimless crime, and therefore necessarily outside conventional economic policy analysis.)

The biblical view of man rests on the presupposition that there are two kinds of people: covenant-breakers and covenant-keepers. There is also such a thing as common grace.[41] When God removes it, people become more consistent with their own ethical presuppositions. Increasing numbers of covenant-breakers turn to crime as an expression of their ethical rebellion against God. The economics of crime and punishment no doubt can be discussed *in part* in terms of criminals' expected costs and benefits, but equally important, if not more important, is the psychological link between crime and certain forms of addiction, especially the addiction to illicit thrills and danger. People's tastes are not stable, contrary to Chicago School economists; people can and do develop an addiction to criminal behavior. They need ever-increasing doses of crime to satisfy their habit. Thus, to analyze all economic actors in terms of the pure logic of expected profit and loss is a fundamental error of modern economic analysis.

Becker disagrees. He wants to consider only people's perceived costs and benefits, risks and rewards, *net*. The logic of Becker's position seems to infer the right of a criminal to inflict damage as heavy as murder so long as he can demonstrate in court through cost-benefit analysis that the particular murder produced net social utility. Coase, writing eight years earlier, was more judicious in his conclusions. He wanted only to assert the right *at some price* of an individual to inflict on other people less permanent forms of damage than murder.

The "Right to Inflict Damage"

Coase considers an example taken from Pigou's *Economics of Welfare*. Suppose that it would pay a railroad firm to run a train

---

41. Gary North, *Dominion and Common Grace: The Biblical Basis of Progress* (Tyler, Texas: Institute for Christian Economics, 1987).

faster than normal, thereby throwing off more sparks. (The example applies to railroads before the era of diesel engines, but it is still valid as an example.) Suppose also that the sparks set a fire that burns a farmer's crop. Pigou said that the railroad company should reimburse the farmer for the loss of his crops by paying him the crop's market value. This, it should be pointed out, is also what Exodus 22:6 says. Coase denies Pigou's conclusion. "The conclusion that it is desirable that the railway should be made liable for the damage it causes is wrong."[42] Why? Because *the economic gains to the total economy*, as revealed by the value of the crops lost vs. the cost of installing spark-arresters on the engine, or the losses to the railroad company if the train was not run at all, *might be greater by allowing the train to emit sparks*. (Might be, might be, might be: How can anyone *know*, given the intellectual tools of modern, subjectivist economics?) The judge should consider the monetary value of the burned crops in relation to the cost of installing a spark-arrester or the monetary losses to the company of running the train more slowly, and then make a decision as to what each party owes the other. In other words, he must consider the *value of total production*. "This question can be resolved by considering what would happen to the value of total production if it were decided to exempt the railway from liability from fire-damage. . . ."[43] Coase argues that it might be better for society in general if the farmer's property rights are ignored, leaving him free to pay the railroad company sufficient money to install the spark-arrester. After all, the value of the crop may be greater than the cost of the spark-arrester.[44]

---

42. Coase, "Social Cost," p. 32.
43. *Ibid.*, p. 33.
44. Clearly, the damage inflicted on the crops planted close to the tracks by numerous farmers could be high. The costs would be high to organize the farmers together in order to contribute money to finance the installation of the spark arrester. Each farmer would tend to wait for the others to put up the money. Each would prefer to become a "free rider" in the transaction: paying nothing, but benefitting from the spark arrester. The payment to the railroad firm probably would not be

What if the farmer had worked for years to build up the soil or build his family's dream home? This labor was unquestionably a manifestation of the dominion covenant. Perhaps he dimly understood that his labor to build the house was in a unique way a moral act under God, meaning his personal conformity to God's injunction to subdue the earth to God's glory (Genesis 1:26-28). The farmer's home is thus not simply a manifestation of his technical competence as a builder; it may also be a manifestation of his self-conscious fulfillment of God's dominion covenant. In other words, his house may be in a very real sense a *holy* thing – a thing *set apart* for God by the very act of constructing it. This is why people are sometimes "irrationally" committed to a piece of ground. A spark-emitting train is threatening his home's existence, meaning the work of his hands, meaning his dream or vision. Is he entitled to no compensation? Isn't the railway *always* liable for damages? Furthermore, if the court decides that the railway is liable – and Coase denies that the court should automatically decide that it is – is the man's shattered dream worth only monetary compensation for the market value of his crops? Maybe he resents the fact that the railway is reducing to mere dollars his right to safety from fire, and market-determined dollars at that. Shouldn't the engines be fitted with a spark retarder, by law? After all, this is not an accidental, occasional incident; this is a daily threat of fire that is a statistically probable event because of the technology involved in running the trains. In short, what about the *psychic costs* to the victim? Coase's analysis completely ignores this fundamental issue.[45]

---

made apart from intervention by the civil government to compel all farmers who are benefitted by the spark arrester to pay their proportional share. The civil government eventually must decide who pays whom: the railroad firm paying damages to the farmers, or the farmers paying "protection money" to the railroad company.

45. This is Walter Block's main criticism: "Coase and Demsetz on Private Property Rights," *Journal of Libertarian Studies*, I, No. 2 (1977).

"Coase, Get Your Cattle Off My Land!"

Or what about the farmer who sees the cattleman move in next door? Or the cattleman who sees the sheepherder move in next door to him? If the other man's animals come roaming into his garden or into his pasture, isn't the victim entitled to compensation? What if the "accident" of wandering animals is not an accident, but a regular way of doing business? Shouldn't the offender be required to put a fence around the wandering beasts? Why should the injured party be required by the court to share the costs of fencing? *Are the victim's property rights of undisturbed ownership not to receive predictable compensation?* What I am arguing, in short, is that the victimized property owner has the right to announce: "Coase, get your cattle off my land!"

My land: there is greater value to me in my right to enjoy my land undisturbed than Coase's reductionist economic analysis indicates. To count the market value of the crops that the cattle trampled, and then to compare that value to society with the meat that someone will put on his table, is *to reduce the value of a man's right of undisturbed ownership to zero*. Coase's concept of social costs ignores one of the most valuable assets offered to men by a free market social order: *the right of the owner to determine who will and who will not have legal access to his property, and on what terms*. To think that monetary compensation for damaged goods at a market price is all that matters to an owner is ridiculous. Rothbard is correct, and I cite his statement again: "There are many problems with this theory. First, income and wealth are important *to the parties involved*, although they might not be to uninvolved economists. It makes a great deal of difference to both of them who has to pay whom. Second, this thesis works only if we deliberately ignore psychological factors. Costs are not only monetary. The farmer might well have an attachment to the orchard far beyond monetary damage. . . . But then the supposed indifference totally breaks down."[46]

---

46. Murray N. Rothbard, "Law, Property Rights, and Air Pollution," *Cato Journal*,

Even more important, there must also be compensation for the loss of security that is necessarily involved in every willful violation of another man's property rights. Exodus 22:5 requires that restitution be paid with "the best" of the violator's field, "and of the best of his own vineyard." To argue, as Coase does, that as far as society is concerned, it is economically irrelevant to the total economic value accruing to society whether the farmer (victim) builds the fence at his expense or the cattleman (violator) does so at his expense is to place zero price on the rights of ownership. *When free market economists place zero economic value on the rights of ownership, they have given away the case for the free market.* This is precisely what Coase and the many academic "economics of law" specialists have done. They have preferred the illusion of value-free economics to the ideal of private property – our legal right to exclude others from using our property.

Theft as a Factor of Production

Coase explicitly argues that the *ability to cause economic injury* is a *factor of production*. Therefore, the State's decision to deny a person the *right* to exercise this ability involves a social cost: the loss of a factor of production. "If factors of production are thought of as rights, it becomes easier to understand that the right to do something which has a harmful effect (such as the creation of smoke, noise, smells, etc.) is also a factor of production. Just as we may use a piece of land in such a way as to prevent someone else from crossing it, or parking his car, or building his house upon it, so we may use it in such a way as to deny him a view or quiet or unpolluted air. The cost of exercising a right (of using a factor of production) is always the loss which is suffered elsewhere in consequence of the exercise of that right – the inability to cross land, to park a car, to build a

---

II (Spring 1982), p. 58.

house, to enjoy a view, to have peace and quiet or to breathe clean air."[47] Coase simply ignores the crucial free market concept that the *legal right to exclude others* from invading your property is *a far more crucial factor of production* – the factor of personal confidence in the honesty and reliability of the civil government. Without this confidence, the free market will be steadily reduced to little more than black market operations.

Coase wants us to "have regard for the total effect" of such uses of our so-called capital, namely, the right to pollute the environment.[48] But "total costs" are precisely what he has deliberately chosen to ignore: *the right to determine whether or not another person can invade my privacy, wake me up at 2:00 A.M., set fire to my crops, send his cattle to eat in my fields, or, ultimately, sell tickets to people to peek through my window at 3:00 A.M.* The economic value of my right to say "Keep your cattle off my land!" – and my right to demand restitution for the violation of this right – is simply ignored by Coase and all those economists who take seriously his economic analysis of social costs. *He offers economic analysis of the right to inflict damage, but he ignores any economic analysis of the right to deny the damage-producer his so-called right.* More than this: *Coase explicitly denies the right of property owners to have their property defended by predictable law, for he says that any consideration of the right to demand compensation depends on "circumstances."*[49] If the right of collecting compensation is not predictable, the right of private property loses its status as a right.

By elevating the "right to inflict damage" to the same level as the right to demand compensation for a violation of a property right, Coase has effectively compromised the latter right by making a potential right out of the ability to inflict damage. *The application of Coase's argument would destroy property rights by attempting to extend the status of property right to a man's ability to*

---

47. Coase, "Social Cost," p. 44.
48. *Idem.*
49. *Ibid.*, p. 21.

damage his neighbor's property. He does not discuss anywhere in the essay *the economic costs to society of compromising the injured party's right to demand and receive by law economic restitution from the offending party.*

Coase does not even seem to understand the implications of his own argument. Most astounding of all, his arguments have been taken seriously by economists who see themselves as defenders of the free market order. Economic reductionism is a very real threat. The more rigorous the logic, the more the threat to real-world policy-making, if this rigor is purchased by the surrender of private property rights, let alone justice.

Transaction Costs at the O.K. Corral

Coase's academic colleague at the University of Chicago, Nobel Prize-winning economist George Stigler, has extended the Coase theorem. Coase argues that in the absence of transaction costs, different initial assignments of property rights will lead to the same economic output. In his authoritative textbook, *The Theory of Price*, Stigler takes this thesis one step farther. He concludes that if there is perfect competition, meaning perfect foreknowledge, market transactions between the polluter and his victim will lead to the production of exactly the same economic output as would have been produced if one firm had owned both the source of pollution and its sink.[50] In other words, the rights of private ownership – the legal right to exclude – and the sense of outrage at an invasion of one's property are economically irrelevant. In a world of perfect competition, amazing things happen. The economic significance of the theft involved in polluting a neighbor's environment is zero.[51]

---

50. George Stigler, *The Theory of Price* (3rd ed.; New York: Macmillan, 1966), p. 113.

51. In complete agreement is Warren G. Nutter, "The Coase Theorem on Social Cost: A Footnote," *Journal of Law & Economics*, XI (Oct. 1968).

All we need is to reduce transaction costs. That should not be too difficult. The polluter can pick up a gun, walk over to his neighbor, put the gun to his head, and force him to deed over his property. Presto: the "internalization" of pollution costs! It will not alter economic output one little bit, Stigler's theory assures us. This surely is a cost-effective way to reduce transaction costs – unless, of course, one's neighbor also has a gun. That, of course, is the whole point.

What possible objection can a self-proclaimed ethically neutral economist offer to this sort of wealth-transfer? This is the question Leff asks in a perceptive critique of the "economics and law" approach to social theory:

> Let us say I am naturally superior to a rich man in taking things, either by my own strength or by organizing aggregations of others (call them governments) to do my will. I am not much of a trader, but I'm one hell of a grabber. That's just the way things are. Is there any way to criticize my activities except from the standpoint of taste (or some other normative proposition)? It would be inefficient to allow violent acquisitions. How can one know that? All of Posner's arguments about the efficiency-inducing effects of private property assume only that someone has the right to use and exclude, not that it be any particular person. If force, organized or not, were admissible as a method of acquisition there is no reason to assume that eventual equilibrium would not be reached, albeit in different hands than it presently rests. After all, as Posner would be the first to tell you, "force" is just an expenditure. If a man is "willing" to pay that price, and the other party is "unwilling" to pay the price of successful counterforce, we have an "efficient" solution.[52]

One Nobel Prize-winning economist who does not ignore the transaction costs of an economic approach to law that elevates efficiency over all other considerations is James Buchanan. In

---

52. Arthur Allen Leff, "Economic Analysis of Law: Some Realism About Nominalism," *Virginia Law Review*, LX (1974), p. 454.

a perceptive law review article, he warned the practitioners of both economics and law that the great benefit which the free market offers society is not its efficiency or its maximizing of economic value. What the free market offers is its support for "institutional alternatives which generate less social tension, less evasion of postulated standards of conduct, more general adherence to legal norms."[53] Yet economists and legal theorists argue that free market economic processes that exist only in an imaginary zero-cost world can and do offer us a cost-effective real-world model: just substitute voluntary market exchanges for enforcement by the State of legal titles. Those who argue this way are not only utopians, they are intellectual arsonists.[54] This is the mid-1960's social philosophy of "Burn, baby, burn!" applied not only to the adjacent field but to society itself.

The Social Costs of the Coase Theorem

There may be a journal essay by a free market economist that has inflicted more damage on the case for economic freedom than Coase's "Problem of Social Cost." There may also be a scholarly essay that has polluted academia's moral environment favoring market choice more than Coase's has. I cannot imagine what that essay might be. (Becker's 1968 essay on "Crime and Punishment: an Economic Approach" comes close, but it is really only an application of Coase's economic approach to law.)

Coase can always argue that his right to inflict such moral damage is merely a factor of academic production. No doubt this essay advanced his academic reputation after 1960. That is what the Nobel Committee believed, in any case. But for every

---

53. Buchanan, "Good Economics – Bad Law," *ibid.*, p. 486.

54. Dahlman is overstating the case against traditional welfare economics when he says that transction costs "are at the heart of the matter of what prevents Pareto optimal bliss from ruling sublime. For if we could only eliminate transaction costs, externalities would be of no consequence. . . ." Carl J. Dahlman, "The Problem of Externality," *Journal of Law & Economics*, XXII (April 1979), p. 161.

benefit there is a cost: that essay surely has inflicted and will continue to inflict damage on human freedom, for it assails the moral case for private property as no article "within the camp" ever has. It has created an intellectually and morally bogus concept of the supposed social economic efficiency of production costs that somehow remain the same, irrespective of the initial distribution of ownership. With that seemingly scientific and academically irresistible conclusion, Coase in 1960 seduced some of the brightest economists and legal theorists of the next generation.

Conclusion

From the day that Lionel Robbins refuted Pigou's defense of the graduated income tax, economists have been confronted with a dilemma: the impossibility of rendering economic judgments scientifically in a world in which it is scientifically impossible to make interpersonal comparisons of subjective utility. The subdiscipline of law and economics is surely a field in which the rendering of judgments is inescapable. The problem raised by Robbins cannot legitimately be avoided, yet it is avoided, and avoided religiously, by the specialists in law and economics.

This subdiscipline can be traced back to Coase's theorem and Becker's essay on crime and punishment. Both of these scholars attempted to strip the subject of normative content. Both of them devised sophisticated arguments in terms of cost-benefit analysis, meaning social costs and benefits. But in doing so, they removed ethics from the rendering of judgment. In Coase's case, he even attempted to prove that a civil judge is not necessary to the rendering of cost-effective judgment. The market can do it all by itself.

These two free market economists have done their best to strip ethics out of both economics and law. But without a moral case for private property, private property will not survive the attacks, political and intellectual, of its ever-present, ever-envious enemies. The weakening of the moral case for the free market is the primary danger posed by "morally neutral" defenses of the free market offered by private property's erstwhile friends. The Coase theorem's threat to the moral integrity of the case for the free society is the reason why the problem of social cost remains a major intellectual problem. The problem of social cost is a lot more difficult than Coase and his disciples have imagined. So is its solution.

6

THE CRISIS: LIVING WITH DIALECTICAL SCHIZOPHRENIA

> *Let us then assume that crises are a necessary precondition for the emergence of novel theories and ask next how scientists respond to their existence. Part of the answer, as obvious as it is important, can be discovered by noting first what scientists never do when confronted by even severe and prolonged anomalies. Though they may begin to lose faith and then to consider alternatives, they do not renounce the paradigm that has led them into crisis. They do not, that is, treat anomalies as counter-instances, though in the vocabulary of philosophy of science that is what they are.*
>
> Thomas Kuhn[1]

Today, most economists appeal "scientifically" to mechanistic explanations of human action. A few go so far as to avoid the use of the word *choice*, since the concept of choice implies a personal decision that is not the result of prior causes. They substitute such phrases as "demonstrated preference." There are a few notable exceptions to this demonstrated preference

---

1. Thomas Kuhn, *The Structure of Scientific Revolutions* (Chicago: University of Chicago Press, 1962), p. 77.

for mechanistic explanations, but these economists are humanistic John the Baptists, crying in the epistemological wilderness.[2]

Typical of the mechanists is Stephen Cheung, a rigorously empirical economist, and rigorously naive technician, who has titled his book, *The Myth of Social Cost*. The book is almost as mythical epistemologically as Coase's original essay. He argues that there is no theoretical barrier against making scientifically valid economic settlements where pollution is involved. He does admit that abstracting from transaction costs does lead to problems. "The important conclusion is that the *solution becomes mechanical once the nature and magnitude of transaction costs, together with other constraints, are sufficiently specified.*"[3] He italicized his words, so he must have regarded them as significant.

What we can and must say, contrary to Professor Cheung, is that *no solution in economics is ever mechanical* because all solutions involve comparisons of subjective value – *inter*personal in the same period of time or across time, or *intra*personal across time.[4] Admit this, and Galbraith's conclusion is inescapable: "In the name of good scientific method he [the economist] is prevented from saying anything."[5] Thus, the modern, "rational" economist is living in an epistemological dream world, a world

---

2. For example, Prof. Kenneth Boulding. See his presidential address to the American Economic Association, "Economics As A Moral Science," *American Economic Review*, LIX (March 1969).

3. Steven N. S. Cheung, *The Myth of Social Cost* (San Francisco: Cato Institute, [1978] 1980), p. 31.

4. On this point – which utterly devastates all humanistic economics, including Austrian subjectivism – see G. L. S. Shackle, *Time in Economics* (Amsterdam: North Holland Pub. Co., 1958), lecture 1; cf. "The Complex Nature of Time as a Concept in Economics," *Economica Internazionale*, VIII, No. 4. Shackle has pushed the logic of pure subjectivism, pure solipsism, and pure autonomy to a preposterous but consistent conclusion: every point in time is unique, incomparable, and autonomous. He calls it the "moment-in-being." For an attempted refutation which fails, see Ludwig Lachmann, *Capital, Expectations, and the Market Process* (Kansas City, Kansas: Sheed Andrews and McMeel, 1977), pp. 81-86. Lachmann falls back on the epistemologically hopeless concept of "common experience" to escape Shackle's logic: p. 86.

5. John Kenneth Galbraith, *The Affluent Society* (Boston: Houghton Mifflin, 1958), p. 150.

of hypothetical scientific neutrality, complex formulas, mathematics, and (usually) taxpayer-financed tenure.

The assumption of ethical neutrality is the essence of what we might call "economic formalism." Pro-free market economists continually appeal to *efficiency apart from equity*. In this respect, Coase is representative of the entire profession. How can we maximize value, they ask, *questions of equity apart*? This is the perhaps the major problem that pro-free market defenders have: overcoming the objections of socialists and other critics of the free market, who point to questions of equity and fairness as the crucial ones, rather than questions of efficiency.

The collapse of the Communist economies has, at least for the present, silenced the socialists. Questions regarding economic efficiency could not be avoided forever; the social costs of socialist economic planning kept rising, even though social costs cannot be measured scientifically according to the epistemology of methodological individualism. But this increase in economic awareness regarding the irrationality of socialism is not the same as a scientific refutation of socialist economic theory. The retreat of the socialists after 1988 was a paradigm shift based overwhelmingly on the public admission by Soviet leaders that the Communist system was not working according to plan, especially five-year plans. It was not the logic of Mises in his 1920 essay on the irrationality of socialist economic calculation that persuaded the socialists;[6] it was Gorbachev's new Party line in 1988. He needed Western credits, and he was willing to admit the economic failure of Communism in order to get them.

Until 1989, the free market's academic defenders generally failed to convince the socialists and ethicists that the benefits of economic efficiency are greater than the social and personal

---

6. Mises, "Economic Calculation in the Socialist Commonwealth" (1920), in F. A. Hayek (ed.), *Collectivist Economic Planning* (London: Routledge & Kegan Paul, [1935] 1963), ch. 3.

costs of competition's "heartlessness," and "economic oppression." Inescapably, the decision as to which is more important – efficiency or morality – is a question of value (subjective and objective), a moral question. But free market economists have so downplayed moral questions in their "scientific" discussions that they are not skilled competitors in any intellectual marketplace of moral ideas. Unfortunately for them, this is the only marketplace of ideas there is. *Because they have emphasized efficiency and have excluded or downplayed questions of morality and value, value-free economists have not been efficient competitors in the intellectual marketplace.* The religion of economic efficiency turns out to be woefully inefficient rhetorically.

Weber's Critique: Dialecticism

Max Weber, the great German social scientist (d. 1920), recognized the tension – a permanent tension, he argued – in all humanistic economic systems between what he called "formal rationality" and "substantive rationality." It is the heart of the debate between capitalism and socialism. It is the question of efficiency vs. ethics.[7] With respect to economic efficiency (for-

---

7. Weber wrote: "A system of economic activity will be called 'formally' rational according to the degree in which the provision for needs, which is essential to every rational economy, is capable of being expressed in numerical, calculable terms, and is so expressed.... The concept is thus unambiguous, at least in the sense that expression in money terms yields the highest degree of formal calculability.... The concept of 'substantive rationality,' on the other hand, is full of ambiguities. It conveys only one element common to all 'substantive' analyses: namely, that they do not restrict themselves to note the purely formal and (relatively) unambiguous fact that action is based on 'goal-oriented' rational calculation with the technically most adequate available methods, but apply certain criteria of ultimate ends, whether they be ethical, political, utilitarian, hedonistic, feudal (*ständisch*), egalitarian, or whatever, and measure the results of the economic action, however formally 'rational' in the sense of correct calculation they may be, against these scales of 'value rationality' or '*substantive* goal rationality.' There is an infinite number of possible value scales for this type of rationality, of which the socialist and communist standards constitute only one group. The latter, although by no means unambiguous in themselves, always involve elements of social justice and equality." Weber, *Economy and Society: An Outline of Interpretive Sociology*, edited by Guenther Roth and Claus Wittich (New

mal rationality), Weber argued, capitalism's socialist critics very often take offense: "All of these [substantively rational, ethical – G.N.] approaches may consider the 'purely formal' rationality of calculation in monetary terms as of quite secondary importance or even as fundamentally inimical to their respective ultimate ends, even before anything has been said about the consequences of the specifically modern calculating attitude."[8] In short, Weber concluded, "Formal and substantive rationality, no matter by what standard the latter is measured, are always in principle separate things, no matter that in many (and under certain very artificial assumptions even in all) cases they may coincide empirically."[9] This assertion of permanent dialectical tension in economic thought was basic to Weber's sociological analysis.[10]

Professional Blindness to Moral Issues

Economists who defend the free market seldom acknowledge the nature of this fundamental debate between the free market's intellectual defenders and the free market's critics. Their "value-free" methodology and their methodological individualism blind them to the realities of the debate – a debate over morality, values, and the effects of voluntary economic transactions on social aggregates. Free market economists cannot seem to understand those scholars and critics who raise the question of individual morality, let alone social consequences and social values, and who then ignore questions of economic efficiency

---

York: Bedminster Press, 1968), pp. 85-86. This is a translation of Weber's posthumous *Wirtschaft und Gesellschaft*, 4th German edition, 1956.

8. *Ibid.*, p. 86. See a slightly different translation of this passage and the one in the preceding footnote in Weber, *The Theory of Social and Economic Organization*, edited by Talcott Parsons (New York: The Free Press, [1947] 1964), pp. 185-86.

9. *Ibid.*, p. 108. [*Theory*, p. 212.]

10. Gary North, "Max Weber: Rationalism, Irrationalism, and the Bureaucratic Cage," in North (ed.), *Foundations of Christian Scholarship: Essays in the Van Til Perspective* (Vallecito, California: Ross House, 1976), pp. 141-46.

for the attainment of the economic goals of individuals. The economists dismiss such criticisms as amateurish and irrational; the fact that most people accept the perspective of the critics does not faze the economists, most of whom see this battle as a technical academic debate rather than a life-and-death war for Western civilization. They see all conflicts as in principle resolvable "at the margin, at some price." They prefer not to discuss the Gulag.

Professional Blindness to Efficiency

Anti-capitalist critics, of course, really do tend to ignore questions of efficiency, a concept which does have to be considered carefully in any relevant discussion of men's economic ability to pursue moral goals, both personal and social. Weber recognized this: "Where a planned economy is radically carried out, it must further accept the inevitable reduction in formal, calculatory rationality which would result from the elimination of money and capital accounting. Substantive and formal (in the sense of exact *calculation*) rationality are, it should be stated again, after all largely distinct problems. This fundamental and, in the last analysis, unavoidable element of irrationality in economic systems is one of the important sources of all 'social' problems, and above all, of the problems of socialism."[11] Thus, Weber pointed to a dialectical tension in all humanistic discussions of social systems. Free market economists and capitalism's critics cannot come to grips with each other's arguments.

The free market economist does have one thing working for him: socialism really is inefficient. People around the globe want the fruits of free market capitalism, which are only too visible on television and in imported media, and steadily national leaders are drastically modifying socialist ownership in order to provide access to these fruits. There is a humorous

---

11. Weber, *E&S*, p. 111. [*Theory*, pp. 214-15.]

definition in the late 1980's that describes the situation in Europe: "Socialist, noun: a capitalist who, for political reasons, cannot admit it publicly." Nevertheless, economic pragmatism is not sufficient to serve as the foundation for an entire civilization. Envy still has a large political constituency.[12] There is a desperate need today for a moral and ultimately religious defense of capitalism.[13] It will not suffice to defend the formal efficiency of the free market by means of an appeal to the formal political techniques of democracy. An appeal to formal rationalism from the market to the election booth and back again is little more than the proverbial pair of drunks who lean on each other in order to stay on their feet. Eventually, they tumble together.

Weber's dualism between substantive rationalism and formal rationalism is as applicable to democratic theory as to market theory. The spirit of democratic capitalism needs moral content derived from outside market theory and democratic theory.[14] The naked public square needs more than the fig leaf of political and religious pluralism to protect it from the socially destructive elements of revolutionary violence and moral erosion.[15] The same can be said for economic theory.

An Alternative to Dualism

The Christian economist who acknowledges the validity of Van Til's epistemology (and who also understands its application) sees no hope in the quest either for a rational ethics – an

---

12. Gonzalo Fernandez de la Mora, *Egalitarian Envy: The Political Foundations of Social Justice*, translated by Antonio T. de Nicholas (New York: Paragon House, 1987), Part B.

13. Paul Johnson, "The moral dilemma confronting capitalism," *Washington Times* (Feb. 21, 1989).

14. Michael Novak, *The Spirit of Democratic Capitalism* (New York: Touchstone, 1982).

15. Richard John Neuhaus, *The Naked Public Square: Religion and Democracy in America* (Grand Rapids, Michigan: Eerdmans, 1984). Cf. Gary North, *Political Polytheism: The Myth of Pluralism* (Tyler, Texas: Institute for Christian Economics, 1989).

ethics supposedly derived from value-free presuppositions (which are mythical anyway) – or the quest for a reliable hypothetical mental construct which in any way relies on the idea of "man, the omniscient." A wholly rational methodological construct along the lines of Parmenides' unchanging logic – with or without mathematics – is apostate man's attempt to find coherence in a changing world apart from God. On the other hand, it is equally fruitless to adopt as one's standard of reference the ideal of "society, the random." Heraclitus' flux is not going to serve as a valid guide to social theory, a kind of Kantian limiting concept against which meaningful reality is measured in a world in which it is impossible to measure interpersonal utility.

General equilibrium theory also cannot serve as a reliable "limiting concept" that judges the performance of a real-world economy of change, responsible decision-making, and uncertainty. The decisions of responsible men cannot be shown to move toward a realm of mankind's omniscience, a world that is peopled (i.e., "unpeopled") with predictable automatons – the underlying assumption of general equilibrium theory. But it is understandable that men who deny God and His providence wish to believe in the potency of such an intellectual construct. It comforts economists. As Ludwig Lachmann wrote in 1943: "Economists, not unnaturally, prefer to do their fieldwork in a pleasant green valley where the population register is exhaustive and everybody is known to live on either the right or the left side of an equation. Only on rare occasions – and scarcely ever of their own free will – do they embark on excursions into the rough uplands of the World of Change to chart the country and to record the folkways of its savage inhabitants; whence they return with grim tales of horror and frustration."[16]

---

16. L. M. Lachmann, "The Role of Expectations in Economics as a Social Science," *Economica*, New Series, Vol. X (February 1943), p. 16. Lachmann is the "Austrian School" economist who has been insistent on the danger of relying heavily on general equilibrium models. "Such smooth transition from one equilibrium (long-run or short-run) to another virtually bars not only discussion of the process in which

Conclusion

The problem for all social theorists is to explain social change in terms of social theory. If we are to make sense of historical change, we need a theory of history. If we are to make sense out of ceaseless economic change, most notably changing prices, we need a theory of economic behavior. This theory must be beyond history yet applicable to history.

The ideal of science has been basic to economic theory from the late seventeenth century. The problem is, the ideal of science (Kant's phenomenal realm) is in dialectical tension with the ideal of freedom and personality (Kant's noumenal realm).[17] So, when the defenders of the free market appeal to economic science as a means of defending the free market, they invoke an ideal that is hostile to freedom. This is a fundamental antinomy of all modern thought, but it is especially glaring in the case of free market economics.

Economics needs the ideal of responsibility as surely as all other social sciences do. Yet this ideal is challenged by the ideal of mechanism. Ethics and efficiency are in dialectical tension in modern thought, including economic thought. What is needed is a reconstruction of economic thought that escapes the dual-

---

we are interested here, but of all true economic processes. . . . And all too soon we shall also allow ourselves to forget that what is of real economic interest are not the equilibria, even if they exist, which is in any case doubtful, but what happens between them." Lachmann, "The Market Economy and the Distribution of Wealth," in Mary Sennholz (ed.), *On Freedom and Free Enterprise*, p. 186. Lachmann's expressed hope in 1956 has not come true – in fact, the reverse has taken place: "It is very much to be hoped that economists in the future will show themselves less inclined than they have been in the past to look for ready-made, but spurious, coherence, and that they will take a greater interest in the variety of ways in which the human mind in action produces coherence out of an initially incoherent situation" (p. 187). Nevertheless, his Kantian individualism, with the human mind serving as the entrepreneurial provider of coherence to an incoherent world, is as impotent to deal epistemologically with the realities of God's creation as are the defenders of general equilibrium theory.

17. Richard Kroner, *Kant's Weltanschauung* (Chicago: University of Chicago Press, [1914] 1956).

ism between the Kantian ideal of science and the Kantian ideal of personality. The dialecticism of modern humanist thought is so deeply rooted that very few scholars, and fewer economists, have dealt forthrightly with the implications of this dialecticism. The endless tension between law and flux, theory and fact, predictability and freedom, and above all, cost and choice has undermined economic thought for over two centuries. Most economists have done their best to ignore this dialectical tension, but inevitably, the problems produced by this tension continue to surface.

Eventually, in a culture-wide crisis, economists will be faced with the reality of their calling. It rests, as does modern thought in general, on a broken epistemological foundation.

CONCLUSION

What is the process by which a new candidate for paradigm replaces its predecessor? Any new interpretation of nature, whether a discovery or a theory, emerges first in the mind of one or a few individuals. It is they who first learn to see science and the world differently, and their ability to make the transition is facilitated by two circumstances that are not common to most other members of their profession. Invariably their attention has been intensely concentrated upon the crisis-provoking problems; usually, in addition, they are men so young or so new to the crisis-ridden field that practice has committed them less deeply than most of their contemporaries to the world view and rules determined by the old paradigm. How are they able, what must they do, to convert the entire profession or the relevant professional subgroup to their way of seeing science and the world? What causes the group to abandon one tradition of normal research in favor of another?

Thomas Kuhn[1]

It may seem odd that I have devoted so much space to the obvious. Unfortunately, economists quite frequently spin complex theories and arguments that are internally consistent – to the extent that arguments are capable of internal consistency[2]

---

1. Thomas Kuhn, *The Structure of Scientific Revolutions* (Chicago: University of Chicago Press, 1962), p. 143.

2. I have in mind the layman's understanding of Gödel's theorem on the impossibility of arguing both completely and consistently.

– but to perform these mental gymnastics, they must ignore, or define away, the obvious. Coase's essay is regarded by many economists as a classic. It is a classic all right – a classic exercise in rarified and misleading sophistry. Yet it is taken very seriously by some of those Chicago School economists who have developed the subdiscipline, "the economics of property rights."

What I argue is that the Bible declares exactly who must pay damages: *the initiator of the damage*. If one man sets a fire, and it spreads to his neighbor's field, he must compensate the neighbor for the accident. If he is an outright arsonist, he is a criminal, and he must pay double restitution – double the market value of the lost crop and equipment. It is not a matter of indifference to the legal system as to who initiated the "nuisance." The Bible does not teach that "from an economic point of view, a situation in which there is 'uncompensated damage done to surrounding woods by sparks from railway engines' is not necessarily undesirable. Whether it is desirable or not depends on the particular circumstances."[3] What the Bible teaches is that the victims of accidental fires must be compensated for their loss. It also teaches that a deliberate violation of another man's property rights is a crime. This is where we must begin any discussion of social costs.

Social costs and social benefits cannot be calculated precisely by means of scientific economics. The economist cannot make interpersonal comparisons of subjective utility, nor can he add up individual utilities or manipulate them by means of some variant of Jeremy Bentham's felicific calculus. We need the Bible to tell us what is right and what is wrong, who pays whom, and whose property should be protected. Society is required by God to adhere to this general principle of justice. The economist has nothing to offer in its place except epistemologically blind intuition.[4] Neither, for that matter, does

---

3. Coase, "Social Cost," p. 34.
4. Gary North, "Economics: From Reason to Intuition," in North (ed.), *Founda-*

the modern legal theorist. Intuition is undefined and undefinable. As the old political slogan says, "you can't beat something with nothing." Men cannot legitimately fight the Bible's definition of property rights with an appeal to circumstances, or to the intuitive ability of men to assess total social costs and total social benefits – especially a total cost package that ignores the right, meaning *legal predictability*, of compensation to the victims.

In the case of the problem of social costs, Pigou's analysis of pollution and restitution was generally in accord with the Bible's discussion of the problem of social cost. The railroad has the legal responsibility to compensate the farmer for any fire it sets. There will undoubtedly be problems for a jury or arbitrator in assessing exactly what the losses were. If the fires continue, then the railroad's officers can be sued for criminal misconduct. Like the man whose ox gains a reputation for goring, but is not penned up by its owner, so are the railroad officers who do not take care to protect people from an identified physical hazard. The formerly docile ox that gores someone to death must be killed (Exodus 21:28). (The engine would at that point be fitted with a spark-arrester or prohibited from the tracks.) But the ox with a bad reputation that kills a man must die, and so must its owner, unless he makes restitution to the heirs of the victim (Exodus 21:29-30). (The directors of the railroad could be held responsible in a court of law for criminal actions for not taking care to install safety equipment after the fire threat had been pointed out to them by the authorities.) Biblical case laws are to govern the courts, not the speculative conclusions of economists that are opposed to the Bible's explicit statements. Sometimes very bright economists can come up with outrageous hypotheses. The public adopts these "logical discoveries" at its peril. Coase's essay is regarded by academic economists – at least non-Keynesian and non-mathematical econo-

---

tions of Christian Scholarship (Vallecito, California: Ross House, 1976).

mists – as a landmark essay. What it is, on the contrary, is clever sophistry: a land mine essay.

The Myth of Value-Free Social Science

In a brilliant yet almost despairing essay, Arthur Allen Leff has described the development of modern legal theory: a war between legal formalism (the "logic of the law") and legal empiricism or positivism ("man announces the law"). The fact is, this debate goes back at least to the Socratic revolution in Greek political thought: the debate over *physis* (nature) and *nomos* (convention).[5] Writes Leff: "While all this was going on, most likely conditioning it in fact, the knowledge of good and evil, as an intellectual subject, was being systematically and effectively destroyed." What he calls the swamp of historical legal studies was replaced by the desert of legal positivism: the "normative thought crawled out of the swamp and died in the desert." He continues:

> There arose a great number of schools of ethics – axiological, materialistic, evolutionary, intuitionist, situational, existentialist, and so on – but they all suffered the same fate: either they were seen to be ultimately premised on some intuition (buttressed or not by nosecounts of those seemingly having the same intuitions) or they were even more arbitrary than that, based solely on some "for the sake of argument" premises. I will put the current situation as sharply and nastily as possible: there is today no way of "proving" that napalming babies is bad except by asserting it (in a louder and louder voice) or by defining it as so, early in one's game, and then later slipping it through, in a whisper, as a conclusion.[6]

---

5. On the rival conceptions of law, see Sheldon Wolin, *Politics and Vision: Continuity and Innovation in Western Political Thought* (Boston: Little, Brown, 1960), pp. 29-34. On *physis*, see Robert A. Nisbet, *Social Change and History: Aspects of the Western Theory of Development* (New York: Oxford University Press, 1969), pp. 21-29.

6. Arthur Allen Leff, "Economic Analysis of Law: Some Realism About Nominalism," *Virginia Law Review*, LX (1974), p. 454.

There is no way for either law or economics to be conducted without an appeal to good and evil, yet it is this appeal, above all, which is prohibited by the methodological standards of modern academic scholarship. The appeal to efficiency by the legal theorists is simply another example of seeking meaningful content for the ethically empty box of legal formalism. When the search for meaning turns to the criteria of economic efficiency, the searchers are being lured down one more dead-end trail. As Leff says, "while you are now working with *is*-terms only (you have escaped the dreaded *ought*), they are, as a matter of fact, very different matters of fact: what indeed *is* of 'value' must be known before one rates the 'efficiency' of getting there. Thus it is possible that all you have ended up doing is substituting for the arbitrariness of ethics the impossibilities of epistemology."[7]

This is the heart of the problem. *Without ethics, there can be no epistemology.* This assertion – which is also a dreaded but inescapable conclusion of modern economics – was the theme that Van Til worked with throughout his career. Economics is a blind science. So is its subdivision, law and economics. Again, Leff zeroes in on the problem faced by the law schools:

> It is a most common experience in law schools to have someone say, of some action or state of events, "how awful," with the clear implication that reversing it will de-awfulize the world to the full extent of the initial awfulness. But the true situation, of course, is that eliminating the "bad" state of affairs will not lead to the opposite of that bad state, but to a third state, neither the bad nor its opposite. That is, before agreeing with any "how awful" critic, one must always ask him the really nasty question, "compared to what?" Moreover, it should be, but often is not, apparent to everyone that the process of moving the world from one state to another is itself costly. If one were not doing *that* with those resources (money, energy, attention), one could be doing

---

7. *Ibid.*, p. 456.

something else, perhaps righting a few different wrongs, a separate pile of "how ghastly's."[8]

Coase himself has admitted as much, though he confines this admission to the narrow confines of the question of transaction costs. "Since property rights can be changed in such a way as to raise as well as lower the costs of transactions, how can one say that a move from regulation to a private property rights system, the use of the market, will necessarily represent an improvement? If the question is put in such a general form, one cannot say that it will."[9] But no one cites Coase's admission.

Christian economists must therefore enter the debate regarding costs, whether social or personal. There is no intellectually consistent way that the humanist economist can legitimately keep Christian economics out of the arena. He has adopted a position of intuitional and arbitrary ethics in the name of value-free methodology. It is all a sham. The more loudly the economist insists that ethics should be left outside the temple of economics, almost as one leaves one's shoes outside a Moslem mosque, the more irrelevant his findings and concealed his own system's ethics. It is better to be open about one's ethics and the source of one's ethics. The reduction of deception, including self-deception, is a legitimate intellectual end. The problem is, neither the embarrassed Christian economist nor the self-deceived humanist economist has been willing to pay the methodological price. But we should have expected this; it is an ancient problem: "Beware lest any man spoil you through philosophy and vain deceit, after the tradition of men, after the rudiments of the world, and not after Christ" (Colossians 2:7).

Economists prefer to avoid thinking about philosophy in general and epistemology in particular. This is what has kept

---

8. *Ibid.*, p. 460.

9. Coase, "The Choice of the Institutional Framework: A Comment," *Journal of Law & Economics*, XVII (October 1974), p. 493.

the crisis at bay. But the epistemological crisis cannot be deferred forever. As Kuhn says, "normal science ultimately leads only to the recognition of anomalies and to crises."[10] But you can't beat something with nothing. "To reject one paradigm without simultaneously substituting another is to reject science itself."[11]

Is there an alternative? I am working on it: biblical economics. It is in the early stages of development. This fact is not necessarily proof of the futility of the project. As Kuhn says, "Often a new paradigm emerges, at least in embryo, before a crisis has developed far or been explicitly recognized."[12] When the looming crisis hits society in general, even academic economists will be under pressure to rethink the epistemological foundations of their calling. Probably not before this culture-wide event, however, for at least three reasons: (1) old habits die hard; (2) tenure is a very conservative force; and (3) the myth of neutrality is today the legal justification for the existence of State-funded universities, which is where most of the world's economists are presently employed.

---

10. Kuhn, *Structure*, p. 121.
11. *Ibid.*, p. 79.
12. *Ibid.*, p. 86.

APPENDIX

THERE'S NO (AUTONOMOUS) ACCOUNTING FOR TASTE

> *For which of you intending to build a tower, sitteth not down first, and counteth the cost, whether he have sufficient to build it. Lest happily [it happen], after he hath laid the foundation, and is not able to finish it, all that behold it begin to mock him, Saying, This man began to build, and was not able to finish (Luke 14:28-30)?*

Having devoted considerable space to what R. H. Coase and modern economists have done wrong, it is time for me to suggest a biblical solution. But before I do this, I need to return to the basic theme of this monograph: the dialecticism of objective and subjective value theory. The dualism between objective and subjective knowledge has always been central to the crisis of non-Christian epistemology, and economic epistemology has not escaped this fundamental antinomy.

Dialecticism arises in modern economics with the issue of imputation. Acting man *imputes* value to a scarce economic resource, be it a stream of income or a course of action. In other words, he makes a *judgment*. It is this act of imputation that lies at the heart of modern, subjectivist economic theory.

Christian economics also begins with the judgment of an acting agent: God. The Christian religion is theocentric. The

Christian analyst is therefore supposed to begin with what God has said and done, as revealed in the Bible. Then he moves to what man says and does. If the issue we are studying is an individual's rendering of judgment, the obvious place to begin is with God's rendering of final judgment.

Final Judgment

The New Testament discusses in much greater detail the final judgment than the Old Testament does. Only one clear-cut reference to the resurrection of the dead appears in the Old Testament, Daniel 12:1-4. This passage speaks of a book sealed for now but which will be opened at the end of time (v. 4). In contrast, the New Testament speaks of God's judgment in terms that can be compared with an account book. We are told that everything we think, say, or do will be publicly reviewed at the final judgment (Matthew 12:35-37). There is a one-to-one relationship between our performance in history and our reward in eternity. The parable of the talents speaks of this relationship in terms of earthly business contracts, but the parable points to final judgment (Matthew 25:15-30). This same performance and reward relationship is spoken of by Paul (I Corinthians 3:12-15).

By placing His own discussion of earthly actions and God's final judgment within the framework of business dealings, Jesus drove home His points in terms of concepts familiar to his listeners. His parables were often either "pocketbook" parables or agricultural parables. Jesus made His point through analogies that would be familiar to people. Those analogies on the surface were economic.

This raises a significant issue: *judgments in history*. Why are men told to "count the cost" of their planned actions? First, because of the threat of economic waste (especially time). Paul warned his readers of the moral necessity of "redeeming the time, because the days are evil" (Ephesians 5:16). Again: "Walk in wisdom toward them that are without, redeeming the time"

(Colossians 4:5). To redeem or buy back the time is basic to the Christian walk before God. The second reason for counting the cost of our decisions is because of the embarrassment suffered by those who fail publicly (Luke 14:29). *The Christian walk is a public walk.* Skeptics are watching the performance of Christians. They will praise or mock Christians in terms of visible performance. Life in the Spirit is therefore life lived in history. We are told in Deuteronomy 4 that the eyes of the world were on Israel. We are told in Matthew 5 (the famous "Sermon on the Mount") that the eyes of the world are on the church; therefore, Christians are not to hide their lights under a basket (v. 5). There is an objective relationship between the *inner life* and *outward performance*. This is what makes accounting possible.

God is the Supreme Judge. He settles all accounts perfectly at the end of time. His standard of judgment is His own law.[1] Man is made in God's image. He, too, has the power to make judgments. He acts as God's representative agent in history, subduing the earth (Genesis 1:26-28). He is not omniscient, as God is, but he has been given the power and therefore the judicial responsibility to think God's thoughts after Him as a creature. *God's judgments are cosmically objective because they are cosmically subjective.* Man's judgments, like God's, are both objective and subjective. They are measured (evaluated) subjectively by God in terms of God's objective law. The point is, *judgments are always personal*; this does not deny their objectivity. It is because man must give an account to God for everything he thinks, says, and does that his imputations are objective.

Judgments and Accounting

The standard textbooks in European economic history say that the development of double entry bookkeeping was a turning point in the history of capitalism, and therefore in Western

---

1. Greg L. Bahnsen, *By This Standard: The Authority of God's Law Today* (Tyler, Texas: Institute for Christian Economics, 1985).

civilization. The technique of recording each financial transaction as both a debit and credit allows the accountant to maintain tight control over all records, and also enables the businessman to identify fiscal hemorrhaging in his business operations. Double entry bookkeeping is an aspect of "man, the judge of history." He is God's agent on earth. He makes evaluations.

Scholars debate endlessly about the dating of this remarkable invention. Standard accounts place it in the year 1340 in Genoa. Scraps of evidence – literally – have turned up indicating that it could have been half a century earlier.[2] The techniques were popularized in 1494 by Luca Pacioli of Venice, as a section of a book on mathematics. Double entry bookkeeping spread throughout Europe, changing every society it touched.

Pacioli also added words of wisdom concerning proper business attitudes and techniques. Clough and Cole quote him:

> Where there is no order there is confusion.
> Every action is determined by the end in view.
> Work should not seem to you strange, for Mars never granted a victory to those who spent their time resting.
> A sage said to the lazy man to take the ant as an example.
> If you are in business and do not know all about it, your money will go like flies, that is, you will lose it.

The authors regard this as evidence of a new spirit of capitalism and rational management in the West.[3] Ludwig von Mises is even more laudatory: "Our civilization is inseparably linked with our methods of economic calculation. It would perish if we were to abandon this most precious intellectual tool of acting.

---

2. Raymond de Roover, "The Development of Accounting prior to Luca Pacioli according to the Account Books of Medieval Merchants," in de Roover, *Business, Banking, and Economic Thought in Late Medieval and Early Modern Europe*, edited by Julius Kirshner (Chicago: University of Chicago Press, 1974).

3. Cited in Shepard Bancroft Clough and Charles Woolsey Cole, *Economic History of Europe* (3rd ed.; Boston: D.C. Heath & Co., 1952), p. 81.

Goethe was right in calling bookkeeping by double entry 'one of the finest inventions of the human mind.' "[4]

The Dialecticism of Humanist Thought

Cornelius Van Til emphasized throughout his long career that modern thought is plagued by an epistemological dualism that can be traced back to Immanuel Kant. Kant divided human life into two radically separate realms, the phenomenal and the noumenal. The phenomenal realm is the realm of scientific calculation, of measurable cause and effect. Effects have specific causes. In this sense, effects are *determined* by their causes. It is this determinism of the phenomenal realm that is the basis of all scientific investigations (except in the subatomic world of quantum mechanics, where there are crucially important effects which have no known or knowable causes – in fact, which are believed by scientists to have no physical causes).[5]

Problem: *in a world of predictable and therefore inescapable physical cause and effect, human freedom disappears*. So does the reality of ethical behavior, given the worldview of humanism, for such behavior is based on the independent (autonomous) existence of freely determined human *choice*. Responsible men are regarded as more than mere biological counting machines. Calculating machines are neither moral nor immoral. They do not choose; they simply respond to inputs according to their humanly designed programs. Kant attempted to salvage both freedom and ethics by positing the existence of an independent (autonomous) noumenal realm of the human personality, or human spirit, which he argued is also the realm of ethical choice. This realm is not under the strict physical determinism

---

4. Ludwig von Mises, *Human Action: A Treatise on Economics* (3rd ed.; Chicago: Regnery, 1966), p. 230. Yale University Press edition (1949), p. 231.

5. Nick Herbert, *Quantum Reality: Beyond the New Physics* (Garden City, New York: Anchor Press/Doubleday, 1985).

that governs the phenomenal realm. The noumenal realm is marked by human freedom and responsibility.[6]

The crucial intellectual problem for the humanist is this: neither Kant nor any philosopher, neither the psychologist nor the social theorist, has been able to describe or explain the epistemologically necessary link between these two realms. To the extent that the noumenal can be classified, defined, and described rationally in terms of the phenomenal realm's logic, it loses its character as a realm of indeterminism. Yet it is this very indeterminism which Kant said must be present in order for the noumenal to be a realm of choice, of human action as distinguished from determined human response. For all post-Kantian thought, *man without the noumenal becomes an automaton.*

Problem: without the ability to think coherently about cause and effect, including ethical cause and effect, man is left adrift in a sea of irrationalism. How can personal responsibility exist in a world of irrationalism? Madmen who break the law or ignore conventions are generally treated as outside the law, and are incarcerated. Thus, the total freedom of the noumenal leads directly to the literal straightjacket of phenomenal judgment and the loss of freedom. The key unanswered problem is this: *How is a man's spirit – his "self" – related to his actions?* Humanist thought has no solution to this crucial moral question.

This problem is not merely a speculative exercise of philosophers. It has inescapable consequences in every area of life, including the science of economics. A crisis in general epistemology produces crises in specific epistemologies. Ultimately, this is a crisis in *ethics*, for ethics in the Kantian worldview is governed (yet somehow not determined) by the noumenal.

Mises and other economists point to rational accounting techniques as the central factor in the development of modern capitalism. Without rational economic calculation, the modern

---

6. Richard Kroner, *Kant's Weltanschauung* (Chicago: University of Chicago Press, [1914] 1956).

division of labor would become impossible. Civilization would collapse. Mises made himself famous with his 1920 essay on the impossibility of rational economic calculation under socialist ownership. Without a competitive free market in goods, especially producer goods, socialist planners cannot make rational decisions about what to produce or what production actually costs.[7] Recent studies indicate that no one has yet refuted Mises on this point.[8] (Socialist economist Robert Heilbroner came to this conclusion in 1990 at the end of his career.)[9]

Economists are fully aware of the crucial importance of scientific accounting methods as the indispensable means of planning, managing, and evaluating economic performance. But modern economists cannot escape the inherent dualism of all post-Kantian thought. They cannot solve this crucial problem: how to relate the inner life of man's self-awareness to the historical realm of cause and effect. Economists have no way to explain how a page full of numbers (phenomenal realm) is related *economically and motivationally* to the decision-making processes (noumenal realm) of rational human beings.

Index Numbers (Continuity)

Take for example the problem of accounting under inflation. Considerable study has been devoted to this topic, especially by free market economists.[10] It is well understood that unexpected inflation leads to capital consumption because businessmen

---

7. Mises, "Economic Calculation in the Socialist Commonwealth" (1920), reprinted in F. A. Hayek (ed.), *Collectivist Economic Planning* (London: Routledge & Kegan Paul, [1935] 1963), ch. 3.

8. Don Lavoie, *National Economic Planning: What Is Left?* (Cambridge, Massachusetts: Ballinger, 1985).

9. Robert Heilbroner, "Reflections: After Communism," *New Yorker* (Sept. 10, 1990), p. 92. It is worth noting that there is not a single reference to Mises in Heilbroner's best-selling textbook in the history of economic thought, *The Worldly Philosophers*. This is an example of how well an academic blackout can work: 1920-1990.

10. This interest increased in the 1970's, when Federal Reserve monetary policy pushed price inflation above 10 percent by the end of the decade.

misinterpret their account books and conclude that capital consumption is in fact profit. Only when it comes time to replace worn-out equipment do they discover that they have made a mistake.

Pierre Goodrich, the multi-millionaire whose money established the Liberty Fund in Indianapolis, made a fortune for his Independent Telephone Company of Indiana by being on the right side of many long-term coal contracts prior to the inflation of the late 1960's and the 1970's. He had been advised by University of Michigan accounting theorist and free market economist William Paton to set up two sets of books, one of which was tied to the government's GNP price deflator.[11] Paton told him to make his decisions on the basis of this "shadow" set of books, not the conventional accounts recommended by his CPA firm (and required by the Federal government). Goodrich for years actually published both sets of books in his company's annual report, the first U.S. corporation to do so. In the early 1970's, companies from across the U.S. ordered a copy of the report to see how it was done.[12]

But there is a major theoretical problem with accounting, a problem more readily understood when we discuss inflation accounting: Who is to say what the "right" commodities are for inclusion into the government's price index? There is more than one available index: wholesale prices, consumer prices, GNP price deflator. The statisticians must assign weighted numerical values to each commodity and service in an attempt to reflect its overall importance to the economy. Question: *Whose* economy? Yours or mine? How can every participant in the economy agree on the proper weights assigned to the selected commodities and services? (Personal evaluations by economists of the economic importance for "the economy at large"

---

11. Paton died in 1990 at age 101.
12. An early Liberty Press publication was *Economic Calculation Under Inflation* (1976), with essays by Solomon Fabricant, William Paton, Paul Grady, George Terborgh, and others.

of a limited number of goods and services are called "weights," which gives you some idea of the problem: a physical term for a psychological phenomenon, meaning a phenomenal term for a noumenal "noumenon.") How can the statisticians be sure which commodities and services should be in the selected list? How important are they, relatively speaking, in the minds of most participants? How do we find out how important an economic good is in the minds of most economic actors?

In constructing their statistical index numbers, the statisticians have to "feel" their way along. They must *intuit* the appropriate weights. But when we use the words "feel" and "intuit," we have returned to Kant's practical reason (the noumenal realm) where numbers determine nothing, and pure reason (the phenomenal realm) is necessarily silent.

How does a decision-maker know for sure that what the account books seem to be telling him is exactly what he wants to know? He cannot be sure, according to subjectivist economic theory. If he is a consistent believer in subjective value theory, he must conclude that all objective price indexes are inherently corrupt and theoretically unjustifiable. He must conclude that any change in the purchasing power of the monetary "unit" cannot in fact be measured in a meaningful subjective manner, for to discuss "purchasing power" you must discuss index numbers of compiled prices, and all index numbers, being aggregates of individual preferences ("weighted averages") are theoretically invalid. Why? Because ever since the classic study by Lionel Robbins, *The Nature and Significance of Economic Science* (1932), economists have known that it is illegitimate to make interpersonal comparisons of subjective utilities. This rules out all index numbers. It also rules out all applied economics, and all economic advice to decision-makers. If taken seriously, this crucial application of subjectivism destroys economics.

Yet these same defenders of subjective economics want to be able to discuss certain relationships. For example, a defender of the "Austrian" monetary theory argues that rising prices are not inflation, but in fact are a result of inflation. Inflation is an increase in the money supply. But what does he mean, "rising prices"? *Which* prices? Gerald P. O'Driscoll, who is presently employed by the Federal Reserve Bank of Dallas, and Sudha R. Shenoy, both of whom are ardent defenders of subjectivist economics, felt compelled to discuss such statistical relationships. They wrote in 1976: "However, after 1945, the problem turned around completely and became that of gently (and later, more rapidly) rising prices. In eleven major developed countries, prices declined hardly at all, and when they did, it was only for a couple of years during the early fifties."[13]

The question arises: How can they know what "prices" – prices in general – did? Because they have statistical evidence. But how did these statistical data come into their possession? Because other economists constructed national index numbers of prices in terms of various *implicitly objective* theories of economics. We are back to the problem of *intuition*, the unstated but crucial basis of modern economics. Kant's dualism remains.

Changing Tastes (Discontinuity)

We also have another problem: *personal tastes that change over time*. What an economic actor thought was a great idea when he began planning may have changed. He may be like the man who stripped naked and leaped onto a cactus plant. When asked later on why he did it, he replied: "It seemed like a good idea at the time." The economic actor originally wanted to achieve one set of goals, but now he has changed his mind. His tastes have changed, and there is no accounting for changing tastes. I mean literally *no accounting*. In fact, most modern economists, but especially "Chicago School" economists, ignore the relevance of changing tastes precisely because changing tastes

---

13. Gerald P. O'Driscoll, Jr. and Sudha R. Shenoy, "Inflation, Recession, and Stagflation," in Edwin G. Dolan (ed.), *The Foundations of Modern Austrian Economics* (Kansas City, Kansas: Sheed & Ward, 1976), p. 186.

cannot be accounted for in their models of economic behavior. Occasionally, some intellectually honest economist will even admit that this is the intellectual game they all play. "Tastes are assumed to be constant because we have absolutely no theory of changes in tastes. . . ."[14]

Thus, the "blank ink" in an account book may no longer tell an individual whether he has been successful or his firm has been successful. It is impossible scientifically to make the connection between *the objective numbers* – entered way back then, when a person's goals were different, his tastes were different, and the purchasing power of money was different – and *a person's present subjective circumstances*. Standards change. For example, the individual who experiences a religious or moral conversion may look at the positive balance sheet (record of the past) in his corruptly operated firm and conclude that the good news on paper is bad news for him (future day of judgment). He interprets the objective numbers from a new point of view.

The problem of the meaning of numerical symbols cannot be deferred at zero cost. But the economics profession defers it.

Systematic Autonomy: Shackling Economic Science

Two economists who have dealt with this problem is considerable detail are G. L. S. Shackle and Ludwig Lachmann. The problem is, when Shackle is finished with his revision of modern economic theory in terms of the logic of pure subjectivism, it is difficult to see what remains of economic science. Shackle begins with the autonomous actor making an autonomous decision, and he ends with the *autonomous moment*. Lachmann summarizes Shackle's position, and then attempts to put the broken pieces together. But Humpty-Dumpty is shattered.

Shackle comes to this extraordinary conclusion: *each subjective moment is self-contained and autonomous*. He calls this the "mo-

---

14. Paul H. Rubin, "The Economics of Crime," in Ralph Andreano and John J. Siegfried (eds.), *The Economics of Crime* (New York: Wiley, 1980), p. 15.

ment-in-being." The entrepreneur looks forward when he makes his plans, and he looks backward when he evaluates the success or failure of his plans, but neither of these actions is scientifically relevant to the "moments-in-being." These autonomous moments-in-being cannot be compared with each other. "Expectation and memory do not provide a means of comparing the actuality of the moment-in-being at one of its stations with that at another, they do not enable two moments, distinct in location on the calendar-axis, to be in being together, for the nature of 'the present,' the essence of the moment-in-being, is an impregnable self-contained isolation."[15] Given the logic of pure subjectivism, Shackle's conclusion is correct.

Lachmann immediately raises the key epistmological question: Can economics survive Shackle's radical discontinuity?

> In other words, in describing the phenomena of human action [no, Shackle was actually describing the *noumena* of human action – G.N.], time cannot be used as a co-ordinate because we lack an identifiable object which "passes through time." Man with his "feelings," preferences, and the content of his consciousness changes in unpredictable fashion. Our author holds that this implies the impossibility of any intertemporal or interpersonal dynamics. His dynamics "seeks to show the internal structure of a single moment," it is "private and subjective." It is valid for an individual at a point in time.

Lachmann then asks: "Is he right in thus confining the scope of dynamic theory?" On the next page, he attempts to salvage something of the science of economics from what little remains of it in Shackle's system of radical temporal discontinuity. He sees where Shackle's exposition leads: to a radical existentialism that borders on nihilism – indeed, has crossed that border.

---

15. Shackle, *Time in Economics* (Amsterdam: North Holland Pub. Co., 1958), p. 16; cited by Lachmann, *Capital, Expectations, and the Market Process: Essays on the Theory of the Market Economy* (Kansas City, Kansas: Sheed Andrews and McMeel, 1977), p. 83.

But if we were to take Professor Shackle's thesis literally, there could be no testing of the success of plans, no plan revision, no comparison between *ex ante* and *ex post*. In fact planned action would make no sense whatever. Nor could there be a market in which the "private and subjective dynamics" of the individuals trading become socially objectified in the form of market prices and quantities of goods exchanged. Common experience tells us that these phenomena do exist. What, then, has gone wrong with our author's thesis?[16]

Better put, *what has gone wrong with humanism's epistemology?* Shackle is being faithful to the dualism of all post-Kantian thought. He is admitting that the *noumena* of "private and subjective dynamics" of acting individuals cannot logically or theoretically become "socially objectified," as Lachmann puts it; that is, they cannot become *phenomena*. Shackle is honest: modern epistemology cannot relate the discontinuous noumena of each subjective decision to a continuous phenomenal (objective cause and effect) system of expectation and memory.

Lachmann suggests that "common experience" tells us that Shackle is incorrect. Indeed it does, but what is "common experience," and how does it relate to scientific economic theory? Lachmann then seeks to find continuity in the system in the human mind. He says that Shackle "comes perilously close" to denying "the continuity of mind." But, I hasten to add, so did Kant, who had to assert the existence of universal categories of human thought in order to preserve coherence for mankind. To escape from Shackle's discontinuity, Lachmann asserts (but does not prove) that man's unchanging mind (continuity) transcends man's changing preferences (discontinuity). "The creative acts of the mind need not be reflected in changing preferences, but they cannot but be reflected in acts grasping experience and constituting objects of knowledge and plans of action.

---

16. Lachmann, *ibid.*, p. 84.

All such acts bear the stamp of the individuality of the actor."[17] Got that? Neither do I. What is he trying to do? He is struggling to reach a conclusion that is required to save economics from radical discontinuity: "Intertemporal comparisons are thus possible except in cases where fundamental changes take place in an individual's system of preferences."[18]

This is like saying that intertemporal comparisons are possible except when they aren't. Who knows for sure whether his own tastes, concepts, or ideas have changed "fundamentally"? Maybe they have changed near-fundamentally. Or maybe he has forgotten what he really believed before. The point is, there is no resting place (continuity) for the autonomous mind if it is to retain its freedom to change (discontinuity) apart from being *determined* by outside forces. But if human freedom is based on indeterminism – and in all post-Kantian thought, it is – then this freedom of decision-making destroys science, for continuity was seen by Kant as an element of determinism (phenomenal cause and effect). If I freely (!) change my mind, am I the same person who established goals before and then began entering accounting data in order to evaluate my success?

"I'm a new man!" says the entrepreneur. Replies his accountant: "Then are these old entries still of any value to you?"

The Kantian realms of the phenomenal (account books) and the noumenal (their meaning to men) are forever separated, yet they must be together if men are to make rational economic calculations. This is the epistemological crisis of economics.

A Christian Answer

We need to defend discontinuity and continuity, subjectivism and objectivism. We need to do this, not out of intellectual necessity alone, but in order to affirm the moral and judicial responsibility of every man and every collective group before

---

17. *Ibid.*, p. 85.
18. *Idem.*

God. As a by-product of a biblical defense of each man's responsibility, we can and must provide the basis of a reconstruction in economic theory. Instead of sneaking objective value theory (continuity) into subjective economic theory through the back door of statistics and index numbers, we must lay as the foundation of economic science both biblical objectivism (God's law) and biblical subjectivism (man's responsibility). Economics must be gounded on an explicitly biblical epistemology. To develop a consistent economic science, we must avoid the dialecticism of both pre-modern and modern epistemology.[19]

We must begin with a covenantal view of God and man. God's covenant has five assertions: the sovereignty of God, the hierarchy of God's authority, the permanence of God's ethical standards, the judgment of God (temporally and eternally), and the continuity through time and eternity of this covenant.[20]

First, we know that God is all-knowing. He can make interpersonal comparisons of all our individual subjective utilities (Luke 21:2-4). Second, we know that we are responsible to God through time. He exercises authority over us. Third, His law is our permanent standard of ethical performance. Fourth, we know that He is the subjective evaluator of all the minds and spirits of every creature in history. We know that he properly "weighs" the importance of every act, service, and commodity. He has objective knowledge of all subjective realities. Fifth, we know that He has a perfect plan for the ages that will be perfectly fulfilled. His people will inherit the earth (Psalm 37:9).

Applying all this to economic theory, we conclude that Shackle's "moments-in-being" are linked through time in terms of God's sovereignty, authority, law, judgments, and plan. Man is made in God's image, so he can make sense of his world. He is personally, covenantally responsible before God, who judges

---

19. Cornelius Van Til, *A Christian Theory of Knowledge* (Nutley, New Jersey: Presbyterian & Reformed, 1969).

20. Ray R. Sutton, *That You May Prosper: Dominion By Covenant* (Tyler, Texas: Institute for Christian Economics, 1987), chaps. 1-5.

our lifetime performance objectively, moment by moment, and also at the day of final judgment. There is objective continuity over time and across interpersonal barriers because man is made in God's image, and God is objectively sovereign.

The God of the Bible is the basis of a theoretical resolution of the subjective-objective dualism of all humanist thought. He is therefore the fundamental presupposition of all valid economics. Without God's comprehensive planning and God's comprehensive judgments (evaluations) through history and in eternity, there is no way theoretically for the economist to "bridge the gap" between subjective value theory and the objective reality of the objective numbers in the capitalist's account books. God is the subjective Author of objective accounting, including index numbers, and man, who is made in God's image, can use accounting techniques to the glory of God and the benefit of society.

Conclusion

The modern economist does not want to deal forthrightly with the fundamental dualism of accounting theory because this problem is a manifestation of the epistemological crisis – the crisis of dialecticism – in humanism's various economic theories. The economist shrugs off such philosophical criticism as peripheral to his task. These epistmological problems have no solutions that are consistent with the economist's presuppositions concerning God, man, law, and time. Therefore, the modern economist concludes that they are irrelevant. He chooses to deal only with problems that may have solutions, and price-competitive solutions at that. So, when his ideological colleagues reach conclusions that sound irrational, immoral, or irrelevant – especially irrelevant – he pays no attention. Irrelevance is par for the academic course. In fact, it is a way of life in the professional journals. Yet economics was announced by its developers to be the most relevant of all academic inquiries: inquiries into the wealth of nations. God is not mocked at zero price.

BIBLIOGRAPHY

Christian Economics

Beisner, E. Calvin. *Prospects for Growth: A Biblical View of Population, Resources, and the Future.* Westchester, Illinois: Crossway Books, 1990.

_____. *Prosperity and Poverty: The Compassionate Use of Resources in a Free Society.* Westchester, Illinois: Crossway Books, 1988.

Chilton, David. *Productive Christians in an Age of Guilt-Manipulators.* Third edition. Tyler, Texas: Institute for Christian Economics, (1985) 1991.

Griffiths, Brian. *The Creation of Wealth.* London: Hodder & Stoughton, 1984.

_____. *Morality and the Market Place.* London: Hodder & Stoughton, 1982.

Hodge, Ian. *Baptized Inflation: A Critique of "Christian" Keynesianism.* Tyler, Texas: Institute for Christian Economics, 1986.

North, Gary. *The Dominion Covenant: Genesis.* Second edition. Tyler, Texas: Institute for Christian Economics, 1987.

_____. "Economics: From Reason to Intuition," *Foundations of Christian Scholarship: Essays in the Van Til Perspective*, edited by Gary North. Vallecito, California: Ross House Books, 1976.

_____. "Free Market Capitalism," *Wealth and Poverty: Four Christian Views*, edited by Robert G. Clouse. Downers Grove, Illinois: InterVarsity Press, 1984.

_____. *Honest Money: The Biblical Blueprint for Money and Banking*. Ft. Worth, Texas: Dominion Press, 1986.

_____. *Inherit the Earth: Biblical Blueprints for Economics*. Ft. Worth, Texas: Dominion Press, 1987.

_____. *An Introduction to Christian Economics*. Nutley, New Jersey: Craig Press, 1973.

_____. *Is the World Running Down?* Tyler, Texas: Institute for Christian Economics, 1988.

_____. *Moses and Pharaoh: Dominion Religion vs. Power Religion*. Tyler, Texas: Institute for Christian Economics, 1985.

_____. *The Sinai Strategy: Economics and the Ten Commandments*. Tyler, Texas: Institute for Christian Economics, 1986.

_____. *Tools of Dominion: The Case Laws of Exodus*. Tyler, Texas: Institute for Christian Economics, 1990.

Rose, Tom. *Economics: The American Economy from a Christian Perspective*. Mercer, Pennsylvania: American Enterprise Publications, 1985.

_____. *Economics: Principles and Policy from a Christian Perspective.* Milford, Michigan: Mott Media, 1977.

Christian Epistemology

North, Gary, editor. *Foundations of Christian Scholarship: Essays in the Van Til Perspective.* Vallecito, California: Ross House Books, 1976.

Rushdoony, Rousas John. *By What Standard? An Analysis of the Philosophy of Cornelius Van Til.* Tyler, Texas: Thoburn Press, (1959) 1983.

Van Til, Cornelius. *A Christian Theory of Knowledge.* Phillipsburgh, New Jersey: Presbyterian & Reformed, 1969.

_____. *The Defense of the Faith.* Revised edition. Phillipsburgh, New Jersey: Presbyterian & Reformed, 1963.

_____. *A Survey of Christian Epistemology.* Den Dulk Foundation, (1932) 1969. Distributed by Presbyterian & Reformed, Phillipsburg, New Jersey.

INDEX

abortion, 31
accounting, 6-7, 9-10, 17, 106-7
addiction, 76
anarcho-capitalists, 34
Austrian School, 28, 53, 56
automatons, 64, 108

Baird, Charles, 1, 68
beauty, 5-6
Becker, Gary
   "criminals," 72
   "crime," 69n
   optional crime, 66
   fines, 68-69
   "harm," 69n
   murder, 73-74, 76
   pin-sticker, 75-76
   prisons, 69
   restitution, 69
Bentham, Jeremy, xi-xii, 73
Block, Walter, 25n
bookkeeping, 10, 10607 (see also accounting)
books, vii
Boulding, Kenneth, 88n
Buchanan, James
   costs (pre- and post-), 5

costs and decisions, 6, 11, 54, 70
efficiency, 84
epistemology, 19
equilibrium, 53n
omniscient observer, 70
price &, 10-11
social costs, 20-21
transactional costs, 83-84
uncertainty, 54
vs. Posner, 29n
welfare economics, 19

Cain, xvi
Calabresi, Guido, 24, 40-45
capital, 10
cause & effect, 108-10, 116
chaos, 16, 70
Chicago School, xv, 26, 27, 39, 43, 45, 47, 70, 75, 98, 113
Cheung, Stephen, 88
choice, 9, 11, 87, 108
Coase, Ronald H.
   cattle vs. crops, 79
   cattleman vs. farmer, 37
   crops vs. meat, 32
   damage, 98

fire & crops, 77-78
free goods, 37
gymnastics, 34
information costs, 37n
intellectual pollution, 27
intellectual pollution, 84
marriage, 47
maximization, 39
"my land," 79
neutrality myth, xvi
Nobel Prize, xiv
Pigou &, 25-26, 76-77
policy-making, 22
pollution, 25
property rights, xv, 39-40, 63, 77, 79, 81-82, 102
publications, 23
reciprocal harm, 30-32
solutions, 39
sophistry, 98
sparks, 77-78, 98
transaction costs, 38-39
Typhoid Mary, 27
weighing gains, 63
Coats, A. W., vii-viii
Coleman, Jules, 38n
common grace, 76
costs
    Buchanan on, 5-6
    comparisons, 1
    decisions &, 70
    immesurable, 5-8
    information, 37
    objective, 6, 8, 21, 53-54
    opportunity, 4-5, 9, 11
    psychological, 37
    Rothbard on, 49-50
    social (see social cost)
    solutions, 39
    subjective, 1
    sunk, 8
    transaction, xv, 26-27, 28-29, 38, 39, 64
covenant, 117
crime, 21, 71-72
criminals, 72-73
crops, 32
cynics, 1-2

Darwinism, 15
demand, 2-3
dialectics, 45
dialecticism, 90-94
Diogenes, 2
distribution, 30
dominion, 78
dualism, 107-9, 115-16, 118
    (see also dialecticism)

economics
    calculation, 109-10
    circular reasoning, 2-3
    dilemma, 21
    equations, 41
    ethics &, xii-xiii, 56, 91-92, 102-3, 109
    formalism, 89, 91
    fraud, 3
    imputation, 104-5
    judgment, 104-5
    intuition, 98-99
    law &, xv, 24, 68, 85
    mathematics, 67
    mechanism, 87
    morality &, 40

Index

neutrality myth, xvi
optimality, 68-69
policy-making, 18-19, 22, 30
predictions, 13
reason, 13-14
relativity, 16
science ?, viii
solutions, 88
tasks, 76
technical, 42
utopianism &, 41-42
value-free ?, 30, 31
welfare, 17, 19, 44
wicked, 31
efficiency
    Buchanan on, 84
    equilibrium, 65
    equity &, 45, 89
    myth of, 50-51
    Rothbard on, 50-51
    social, 33, 50-51
Egger, John, 1
envy, 93
epistemology
    ethics &, 101
    lack of interest, 19
    only you!, 4
    resentment toward, viii-ix
    Robbins vs. Harrod, x-xiv, 17-19
    self-interest, ix-x
equations, 41
equilibrium, 53, 57-58, 64, 65, 67, 94
equity (see justice)
ethics
    appeal to, xii-xiii
    economics &, 102-103, 109
    epistemoloty &, 101
externalities, xiv, 25-26
    (see also pollution)

fines, 68-69
fire, 98-99
flux, 52, 95
free market, 93
freedom, 107, 116
Friedman, Milton, 13n

Galbraith, J. K., 88n
games, 29-30
genocide, 31, 55
Georgescu-Roegen, Nicholas, 16
God, 7-8, 31, 47, 58, 65, 76, 98, 117-18
Goodrich, Pierre, 110
grace, 76
gunnery sergeant, 43

Halévy, Elie, xi
hall of mirrors, 44-45
Hardin, Garrett, 46
harm, 30-32, 69n
Harper, F. A., 57n
Harrod, Roy, x-xiv, 17-19, 51-52
Heibroner, Robert, xiv, 109
Heraclitus, 16, 59, 94
Humanist Manifesto, 15n

ideal type, 57
imputation, 8, 104-5
indeterminism, 108, 116

index number, 110-13
inflation, 110-12
institution, 45
intuition, 67, 98-99, 111

Jewish law, 26
journals, vii
judge, 85
judges, 21, 27, 28,, 33, 38, 42-43
judgment, 104-7
justice
   cost of, 31
   economics &, 56
   efficiency &, 45
   ignored, 39-40
   sense of, 37
   violating, 65

Kant, Immanuel, 95-96, 107-8, 115
Keynes, J. N., 18n
kidnapping, 31
Kuhn, Thomas
   anomalies, 87, 103
   anomaly, 36
   books, vii
   common sense, vi
   loss of faith, 87
   malfunction, 13
   neutrality, 23
   new paradigm, 48
   normal science, vi
   paradigm, 38
   paradigm game, 63
   paradigm shift, 97
   professionalization, vi

Lachmann, Ludwig, 88n, 94, 114-16
land, 79
law
   battle, 100-102
   biblical, 68
   economics, 68
   economics &, xv, 24, 85
Leff, Arthur, 29n, 83, 100-102
Lehn, Kenneth, xiv-xv
Letwin, William, 71
Levine, Aaron, 26, 46-47
Lewin, Peter, 33-34, 65
Liberty Fund, 110

Machlup, Fritz, ix
man, 15
market order, 10
marriage, 5, 29-30, 36, 47
mathematics, vii, 6, 67
measurement, 1, 5-8, 11, 14-16, 21, 40
methodology, viii, 57-59
Mises, Ludwig von
   accounting, 107-8
   action, 58
   evenly rotating economy, 58-59
   methodology, 59-60
   socialism, xiv, 57n, 89, 110
   utilitarian, 57n
   variables, 15n
Mitchell, John, 30
money, 29
murder, 73-74, 76

Index

neutrality, xvi, 40
numbers, 6-7, 110-12

O'Driscoll, Gerald, 112
omniscience, 41, 60n, 70, 82, 94
ownership, 30
ox, 99

Pacioli, Luca, 107, 119
Pareto, V., 42n
Parmenides, 16, 59, 94
Paton, William, 110
Pigou, A.C., 17, 20, 25-26, 76-77, 99
pin-sticker, 75-76
policy-making, 52, 54 (see also Robbins)
political science, xiii
pollution
    appropriate level, 21
    Coase's essay, 25
    externalities, 25-26
    solution, 88
    Pigou's view, 20
    Stigler & Coase, 82
    subjective value theory, 12
Posner, Richard, 1, 24, 28-29, 74n, 83
possibility, 10-11
price, 2-4, 10
prisons, 69
property rights
    bundle of rights, 37
    Coase on, xv, 39-40, 63, 77, 79, 81-82, 102
    enforceable, 38
    exclusion, 36
    value of, 39-40, 63, 82
Protagoras, 15
punishment, 21

railroad, 99
reason, 13-14
Regan, Donald, 38
relativity, 15-16
responsibility, 98, 106, 117
restitution, 69, 80, 98
Rizzo, Mario, 53
Robbins, Lionel, x-xiv, 17-19, 85, 112
Rothbard, Murray N.
    damages, 79
    efficiency, 50-51
    ethics, 56
    farmer & railroad, 49-50
    policy-making, 52
    social cost, 48
    utilitarianism, 54-55
Rubin, Paul, 72n

scarcity, 43
science
    economics, viii
    psientific, 68
    sacred law, vii
Shackle, G. L. S., 88n, 114-16
Shenoy, Sudha, 112
Siegfried, John, vii
Smith, Adam, 14
social change, 95
social cost
    Becker on, 71-72
    denial of, 33, 48-49

efficiency, 33
ethical problem, 30
God's hustice, 98
Lewin on, 33
market failure, 20
Pigou, 20
pollution, 20
social order, 47
social theory, 95
social value, 18
social wealth, 29
socialism, 89-91, 92, 110
society, 3, 16
sociology, xiii-xvi
sparks (train), 77-78
speed of light, 15
Stigler, George, 75n, 82
stock market, 10
subjectivism, xi-xiv, 17-19, chap. 4
suicide, 16-17
sunk costs, 8
supply, 2-3

tastes, 76, 113
taxation, 17, 19, 85
Thirlby, G. F., 9-10, 70
transaction costs, xv, 26-27, 28-29, 38-39, 64

Typhoid Mary, 27

uncertainty, 50-51, 54
utilitarianism, 25, 54-55
utilities, 1
utility, x-xiv, 17-18, 21, 28, 30, 32, 34, 40, 85
utopianism, 41-42

value
   changing, 51, 104
   imputed, 8, 14
   neurality &, 40
   objective vs. subjective, 104
   scale, 21
   subjective, 5-8, 14, 17-19, chap. 4
Van Til, Cornelius, 52-53, 59, 93-94, 101, 107

water-diamond paradox, 14
wealth, 29
Weber, Max
   dialecticism, 90-94
   ideal type, 57n
   rationality, 90-92
welfare economics, 17, 19, 44